Spread the
Love!

Brigitte
Berman

Dorie

Dorie

Dorie

Dorie

Dorie

Dorie

Dorie

Dorie

Dorie

Dorie Witt's Guide to Surviving Bullies

Brigitte Berman

DORIE WITT'S GUIDE TO SURVIVING BULLIES
by
Brigitte Berman

This book is published by Dorie Witt Books and printed in the USA.

FIRST EDITION: 2009

Jacket art copyright © 2009 by Howie Green
All rights reserved.

Interior Layout: Pam Marin-Kingsley, Far-Angel Design
Cover layout: Cathy Colbert

ISBN: 978-0-578-00927-8

Library of Congress Registration Number: TXU1-595-020

Visit Dorie on the web at: doriewitt.com

I dedicate this book to my mother and father who gave me the encouragement to pursue my dreams; my sister Margot, who would never let me forget it if I didn't, and most importantly, put up with my crazy and sporadic writing schedule. Also Patti Jones, without her help I would still be sitting on the dock writing because she was my mentor and she encouraged me and made this book possible. Howie Green, who is the best and most patient artist I have ever met and who brought Dorie to life; and let's not forget my school for giving me the education to write this book; my good friends who supported me and took my questionnaire and survey, and you, dear reader, and all other teens who have suffered from bullying.

ALARM WILL SOUND

beep, beep, beep, beep

PRIVATE! PRIVATE!

WARNING!

P.S. I can hear the alarm!
(super sonic hearing)

LUNA, GO NO FURTHER!!

OK EISE......I'll tell mom!

TABLE OF CONTENTS

Dear Diary and Readers,

The following is the top secret, confidential, diary of Dorie Witt, i.e., me! If you, the reader, are not Dorie Witt or have not been granted permission to read the diary from me, then you are a snooper. If you are a snooper, I would like you to return the diary to my bedroom after you have completed reading it because I will need my diary soon. Also, I would ask you snoopers to stop snooping, but this request would probably make you want to read my diary even more. Besides, if you were nosing around my bedroom, you obviously haven't heard of personal space and a diary is very personal space! It's all right though, I forgive you. If you see something you don't like, I'm sorry, but that's not my fault. After all, this is a diary; what do you expect? As you will soon find out, this isn't a normal diary. For the benefit of all

you nosy pants who are reading this right now, let me explain how my diary works. This particular diary is my survival guide to bullying, a topic everywhere in our world today. The mass media is covered with stories about teenage bullying and if you haven't heard the news, all you have to do is turn on the television, open a magazine or read the newspaper.

I have personally been bullied for reasons I do not understand and have had trouble understanding the twisted minds of these bullies. So, to better understand bullying and other social challenges of our time, I have interviewed a large variety of people from many different schools and many different lifestyles with a questionnaire. Some of my school mates don't understand why I want to know more about these issues and think I'm weird, but that's their problem, not mine! After reviewing all the data collected from my questionnaires, I realized that I'm not the only one who has been bullied and taken advantage of by people and situations. The problem is everywhere!

At the beginning of each chapter under **Your Two Cents**, you'll find actual questions from my questionnaire and answers provided by my survey takers. By the way, my survey takers are middle school and high school students with a variety of personalities and lifestyles. You will also find a small fact about bullying under **The Real Deal**.

This is just a tidbit of information for you to think about as you read the story. Also, at the end of each chapter I discuss the issues and problems from the chapter in **Dorie's Two Cents** and try to give helpful advice. It's a wiser version of me writing about things I have learned. Dear Diary Reader, this is for you and I hope **Dorie's Two Cents** provides support and ideas for coping with problems you nosey pants may have experienced in and out of school.

Middle school and high school years can be very difficult to survive and if what I've learned can be helpful, you are welcome to read this diary and pass it on (excluding Luna, my sister). One more thought before you get started. Dear Diary Reader, you can get through these tough years!! Remember, middle school and high school years are only 7 years of your life. It may seem like a lot, but the average women lives to be around 80 years old! Flies by pretty fast, eh? Hang in there, I'm here for you!!! Shall we begin?

Dorie

CHAPTER 1
THE NIGHT BEFORE SCHOOL JITTERS . . .

THE REAL DEAL

Children and youth who are bullied are typically anxious, insecure and cautious. (NYVPRC)

YOUR TWO CENTS

Question 1: Do you get nervous very often and how do you feel?
Response: "Sometimes I get nervous when I'm doing something new. I always start feeling bad about myself and then I have to keep reminding myself that everything will be fine."
Question 2: How do you survive being nervous?
Response: "I take deep breathes in and out and this usually calms me down."

me, too!

Dear Diary,

I have the "night before school jitters." I'm excited and terrified at the same time. Is that even possible? I have to pick out an outfit, but I'm not sure what to wear. What you wear on the first day of school sets a standard of what you're going to wear for the rest of the year. If I dress preppy; I'm preppy; if I dress punk; I'm punk. Maybe if I combine everything together, I won't be labeled a certain style. Then again, I could be labeled as fashionably challenged and extremely weird. Sounds like a bad idea, because if I do this, the rest of the year I will be teased. Don't want that. In the past, I have been the one who everyone picks on. It's usually because of the way I dress. I do agree that I have a unique style at times, but that doesn't mean others have the right to critique what I like to wear. Whatever, I'll just ignore the comments! It's not as if there are cute boys at my school I want to impress, but then again, I have spent the whole summer in the middle of nowhere at our family's lake cottage "family bonding."

Don't ask; it wasn't my idea, it was my parents. They said, "A family needs time away from all of the busyness of life to really get to know each other and talk; time to bond." Who said parents knew what they were talking about and my family is, how should I put it...weird. Unlike other moms, my mom feels that she needs to be an "active ingredient" in our lives and yes, she did say "ingredient." To her this means being "interested and involved," to me it's being nosy. Everyday when I came home from school last year she would ask me, "How was your day?" and it wouldn't stop there. You would think if I said "fine" she would buzz off, but I was not to be so fortunate. She would prod me with random questions: "Why was your day fine?" Are you keeping up with your school work?" "Any cute boys?" Oh my goodness, it was so annoying!!! I think she's overly

mom

interested in my life because she doesn't have one of her own. Just food for thought, but don't tell her I said anything because I wouldn't want to hurt her feelings. Mom has blonde hair like mine, cut just above her ears with short bangs. I don't really like the hair

cut and it went out of style twenty years ago, but it's her head not mine. She is a good Mom and I know she cares about me, but she drives me crazy when she tries to be funny, especially in front of my friends. I wonder when she'll catch on her so called "jokes" aren't funny. For example, one time I had a really busy week, so I didn't have a chance to clean up my bedroom. We were carpooling with an acquaintance and the two of us went to my bedroom to grab something I forgot. Mom turned to my friend and said, "Warning, be careful, Dorie's room looks like a video game underwear obstacle course." Way to go with the joke, Mom. Talk about mortifying!!!!! To make matters worse, Mom ends her little dig with a snorting kind of laugh. She sounded exactly like a hyena!! Let's just say we haven't carpooled with many friends since the underwear laugh!

I think my father would be interested in my life if he could hear, but talking to him is like talking to a brick wall. Somehow it is really soothing though, because he always says what you want to hear so no one gets upset. Because of my father's lack of hearing, there is often much controversy when we go to a crowded place. Let's just say, he is easily confused (since he can't hear) and this can lead to a lot of embarrassment for the whole family (excluding him; he doesn't know he's embarrassing us).

Also, we like to play practical jokes in my family and my father's jokes tend to be extremely embarrassing, partly because he thinks he's funny…but he's not. So we like to really get back at him when we can. My sister, Luna, and I played a really great prank on him last winter. Dad's hair has long since turned gray and is thinning by the day (I guess this is normal for a 48 year old, isn't it?). We found an old rabbit fur hat in the attic which was shedding like crazy. We realized the fur was the same color as my dad's hair, gray of course, and we decided to gift wrap the hat and give it to him as "a present." When we gave it to him, he thanked us and said he would wear it right away. The next day, he wore his hat when he was supervising Luna and me shoveling the driveway. Halfway through the job, Sergeant Daddy said we could have a break, so we went back into the house for some hot cocoa. Sure enough, Luna and I

noticed little gray hairs all over his coat because the rabbit hat was shedding. We started asking, "Hey, Daddy, what's wrong with your coat, there are gray hairs all over it?" For a few minutes, he actually believed his hair was falling out and we thought he was going to go crazy. Sadly, Mom walked into the room and showed some logic by

pointing out it was his rabbit fur hat. Luna and I were in trouble big time for the practical joke, but it was definitely worth it. Just the look on his face when he thought his hair was falling out so fast was priceless. After that, my mom put a halt on our practical jokes because she said somebody could get hurt. Also, if she found us breaking the new rule, she would disconnect all the televisions in the house for the rest of the year. Obviously, nobody has broken the rule.

My sister Luna...do not get me started... she is so obnoxious!!!! It seems everything I like she dislikes. I love country, rock, pop, classical and some oldies music. In fact, I like almost all music, except the songs Luna picks out. She enjoys listening to rap, Frank Sinatra and the Beach Boys. I can only take so much "fun, fun, fun, till my daddy takes the T-Bird away." I DID like the song until it came blasting from my sister's iPod speakers every single night, as if the repeat button was stuck. This

summer we drove my mom crazy with our music wars. Luna would turn her music up loud just to annoy me, so I would turn my music up louder. The music became so loud we were banned from using our speakers at all for one whole week. Let's just say, there were many weeks we couldn't use our speakers.

Luna is two years younger than I and looks like she just stepped out of a Ralph Lauren or Lacoste Catalogue. One word to describe my little sister, besides "abnormal," is "PREPPY." She enjoys wearing skinny jeans, collared shirts (with popped collars of course), while I love to wear bright colors, wild designs, tons of jewelry and often not caring to match any of the above. I consider myself to be her exact opposite and this idea is the only thing we seem to agree on. Luna does have her good moments, but we seem to be fighting more than not. I guess it's normal for sisters to fight sometimes and maybe if we weren't so different, we would be better friends. Even though it pains me to say this, at times, I do in fact enjoy her company.

Luna is rather petite; she is around five feet five inches tall while I seem to be a monster next to her. I tower over her like Godzilla at a whopping five feet ten inches. Five feet ten inches isn't exactly all THAT tall, but it's embarrassing when people talk about my height as if it's so odd and then try to persuade me to play basketball, assuming I would have such an advantage. Once they see me flopping all over the basketball court, it wouldn't matter if I was fifty feet tall, they no longer want me on the team. That's ok though; I'm not really into sports. Let's just say, I'm not very athletic and I can accept this fact.

In direct contrast, Luna defies gravity, especially when she is golfing. Who knew someone so small could send a golf ball flying two hundred fifty feet into the air?!! It was really funny when Dad took her golfing for the first time and told her it's ok if she doesn't do well. A natural athlete… she whipped his butt!! Now he asks HER for golfing advice, although he will never admit it. Luna's obsession with golf influences the way she dresses. If I were a complete stranger and saw her walking down the street, I would instantly know she was a golfer by her attire; a lot of plaid and popped collars.

Luna

Luna has really long, wavy brown hair with natural blond highlights and it has tons, and I mean tons, of volume. In a movie theater, you definitely don't want to be the person sitting behind her because you won't

see the movie, only the volume of all her hair. We went to a theme park this summer and it was really fun, except for one reason. Whenever we went on a fast ride and she sat in front of me, her massive hair kept blowing backwards, whipping my face and blocking my view. It could have been really dangerous because I couldn't see a thing and had no idea what was coming up next. Worst of all and pretty disgusting, was having to deal with her hair in my lip gloss during the rides. Talk about gross!!! I brushed and flossed my teeth for almost an hour when we arrived home. You can image how annoyed Luna becomes when we make fun of her naturally large and "unique" hair.

My hair is completely different from Luna's because it is blonde and rather straight. I like my hair, but sometimes I wish it had a little more bounce. Whenever I add styling products to at-tempt volume, I end up with stiff, rigid hair instead of the "luscious bouncy locks" they advertise on television. Don't get me wrong, I love my hair, it's just depressing I have to work so hard to add so

little volume and I still can't master the look! During the summer, I decided to change my hair and added pink highlights. My mother thought the change was "interesting," but Luna smirks when she looks at my rosy hair. It doesn't matter what anyone thinks, I really like it and the pink adds "character!"

I also have two older brothers, but they are geezers. They're in

college right now and on the opposite side of the coun-try. They can't afford to come home often, so we don't see them too much, which is not a problem for me. Having them away bothers my mom though, because she really misses them. I will admit that at times I do miss them, but don't let anyone know; it would ruin my reputation. Some people (my best friend, Alana, for example) say my brothers are VERY handsome. I beg to differ! My brothers are two years apart (one is 20; the other is 22) but they might as well be twins since they look and act alike. Both enjoy the look of skinny jeans, guy scarves and graphic tees, and they also have those dreamy blue eyes and shaggy brown hairstyles most girls my age would consider "irresistible." I seem to be resisting pretty well, but then again, how could I get it? After all, I AM their sister.

OMG!!!! I have just wasted way too much time writing about my family. I am such a dork! I should be picking my outfit for the first day of school. Like I said, I am really nervous and have to figure out the perfect outfit to wear. I don't want to make the wrong impression on the first day! I really made a fool of myself at the end of school last year, so people are going to start the year thinking I'm a dork; I don't need to continue this train of thought! At the end of last year, we had a class pool party and I wore my favorite bikini with cute monkey logos and ruffles. Many of my classmates thought it was ugly and they were making fun of me big time. When I went to jump into the pool, this guy who thinks he's so funny, when actually he is a bully, pulled the string of my bikini top so the knot came undone. I came out of the water unaware that my bathing suit top was floating next to me! I was humiliated beyond belief, so I need to start this new school year with better style. I am tired of being bullied so my clothing choices must be right. I'm thinking

about wearing my bandana…it could be perfect. I wonder where my bandana is. I can't go to school without it!! OMG! Where is it? If it's not in my room, there is only one place it can be. I storm out of my bedroom and across the hall to where my arch foe, Luna, resides and continually plots her next move to drive me further to the edge of insanity. I raise my fist to pound on the door when my little sister opens it. Note to Luna: if she keeps opening the door when I am in the midst of a knock, she's going to be accidentally hit in the face one of these times.

Luna w/ a beard

"What do you want?" she asks in a demanding tone.

"Well, aren't we friendly today," I retort.

"I was in the middle of an important clothing decision; could you make it snappy?" she barks.

me

Luna
upset at

Even though it may appear she was making a request, I can assure you, it came out like a command. Things must not be going well in preppy polo heaven! I look at her a minute, taking my time, pretending I didn't hear her comment about making it snappy. She raises her eyebrows. Watching her facial expressions can be so much fun! Dear Diary, observe the ancient art of annoying an impatient sibling!

"Do (long pause by me) you (another long pause with an exasperated sigh) have (another pause in which I pretend to be deep in thought about my question) my (these long pauses are driving her crazy, Diary if only you could see it) bandana?" I say extremely slowly just to add effect.

"I sent it to What-Not-to-Wear." she blurts out.

I exclaim, "Very funny. Now hand it over!" but Luna spits,

"Yuck! You actually think I would want that thing? I would never want to dress like you; it would be social suicide."

"Wow, you're so kind!" I say in a very sarcastic manner.

"I know," she says. I glare at her for a moment before deciding to go find Mom. If anyone knows where my bandana is, it's Mom. I find her knitting in the living room; it's one of her new hobbies and she looks comfy sitting in her favorite armchair by the television. Mom is wearing her usual high-waisted old lady jeans, black t-shirt and white tennis shoes.

"Mom, do you know where my bandana is?" I ask her.

She doesn't look up from her knitting, "You mean the thing you tied on your arm this summer?"

"Yes, that," I say and think, what else would it be?

She continues, "I brought it with me to the sporting goods store so I could buy one like it, it's so cute!" I just stare at her

with my mouth hanging open like one of those cartoon characters. I cannot believe she wore my bandana!!!!!

"Goodnight, Mom," I say dejectedly and walk upstairs. I am in shock. If my mom thinks my bandanas are cute, they must be dorky. If I wore something all summer my mother likes, this makes me a dork. This is a disaster! Thank goodness I didn't wear my bandana to school, because it would be another end of the year pool party scene all over again! Why does my mom always have to start wearing things I wear?? Doesn't she realize I am made fun of for my style of dress? If she knew, I bet she would never wear something I have worn

ever again!!! Also, why do people think I have such bad fashion sense? Did they ever think I just like to dress differently from others? Instead of trying to fit in, I try to stand out with my own style. Is there something so wrong with being different; am I doomed to be made fun of forever because of my apparently "odd" fashion beliefs? Now I'm going to have to burn my bandanas; what a shame, I rather liked the way they looked. Now my whole outfit plan is ruined! I better call in reinforcements.

I go downstairs, grab the portable phone, and bring it to my room. For some strange reason, I'm not allowed to have a phone or computer in my room, which is completely ridiculous because I spend most of my life on the phone. Parents, no one can understand them; I don't think they even understand themselves. Whatever, I'm not going to try to figure parents out right now, it would take too long.

Back to the current crisis: MY OUTFIT! I think I'll call Alana and Cass because I'm not in the right frame of mind to talk to anyone else. Moreover, they ARE my best friends in the whole world so Diary, I need to tell you about them because I know you wouldn't want me to ramble on about someone you know nothing about.

Alana has long, almost black hair, with waves down to the middle of her back. It's really pretty and

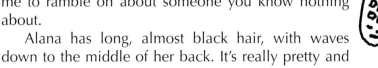

looks great with her blue eyes. She dresses preppy hippy, wearing polo t-shirts with jean skirts, flat shoes and chunky jewelry. It wouldn't be surprising to see her with a thin stretchy headband around her forehead, instead of on top of her head. I know this sounds rather preppy, but preppy is a word reserved for my sister so I have to use another word to describe Alana; I think preppy hippy does the trick.

Prep

As much as I love Alana, I get annoyed with her because she can be completely tactless. She just blurts things out about people, even when they are standing right next to her!! Because she's so pretty, she doesn't really know what it's like to be teased and tormented. The Popular Clique at school absolutely hates her because she is such a threat to their imagined popularity scale...or so I've heard. I think they feel threatened about Alana because THEY want to be known as being the prettiest people in school. The Populars probably think if the rest of the kids at school start commenting on how pretty Alana is, then they won't be popular anymore.

we hate Alana

Maybe I'm just a tad bit envious of her looks, but sometimes Alana appears so vain and uncaring about the feelings of others and it really drives me crazy. Last year I was flirting with some really cute guys and she came to join me in the conversation. I'm pretty sure they were

me pulling my hair out!

becoming interested in us when she decided to tell one of them he needed a new haircut. Who tells someone to get a new haircut, especially a cute guy!! She completely ruined our chances with them and this was not the first time!!! I wonder if this has anything to do with how pretty she is, does she feel entitled to be so brash? She IS my best friend though, so I try to focus on the things I like about her. Alana is really funny and is honest if you ask her a question. She's also fiercely loyal and I don't know what I would do without her friendship. We met in second grade when we fought about something silly and the teacher made us sit out of recess; we bonded and have been friends ever since. We sure go back a long time, in fact, we have been virtually inseparable all these years!!

Then Cass came into the picture. Cass has really red, curly hair, cut right above her shoulders. According to her, her hair is really dark auburn. I think it's red, but whatever, it looks really pretty.

Cass thinks her hair is an explosion of frizziness. Alana and I correct her; it's just very full, not voluminous like Luna's, and only full in an outwardly expanding manner. Cass also has really cute red freckles on her nose and dark brown eyes. She usually wears clothing from stores like Aeropostle and American Eagle, which is how most people in our school dress. Unlike Alana and me, Cass doesn't like to experiment with her clothing and we sometimes embarrass her with our wild choices in outfits. Whatever, we don't care how we look, so Cass just has to deal with our unusual style. In fifth grade, Alana and I met Cass when she moved from California and we became her first friends; the rest is history. The three of are now like one mind; i.e., we know everything about each other and can finish each other's sentences.

Forget passing notes in class, one glance and we know each other's thoughts. The only problem I have with our friendship is Mom warns me to be careful around Cass; she thinks Cass appears to be dishonest sometimes. I know Mom has my best interests at heart, but sometimes she can be such a worrywart. I try to take her opinions and give them a little bit of thought and attention before discarding them, but in the back of my mind, there is a nagging feeling she's right, but what if she's wrong?

I'm going to call Cass first because she almost always answers the phone and has a great flair for style...but...how weird...Cass isn't picking up and I have an outfit crisis! I guess I'll have to make do with a one-person judging panel, Alana. I press speed dial for Alana's number, "Ughhh! Why does it always take her so long to pick up the phone?" I ask myself. Finally, a "hello" comes from the other end of the line.

"Hey, it's me," I say.

"Me as in you, or me as in me?" Seriously, could she use her advanced mathematical brain anywhere else besides in math class? I don't understand. Besides being beautiful, Alana can solve any math problem in less than 10 seconds flat, but when it comes to common sense…let's just say she is a tad bit lacking.

"Me, as in your best friend Dorie!!!!"

"Oh, what's up?" she asks.

"I'm having a clothing crisis!" I whine.

"Oh, that stinks," she replies. Excuse me, this is the time when friends are supposed to comfort you, not state the obvious!

"HELLO, this is an emergency!" I say.

"Why don't you just wear the cute new top you bought the other day to match your bandana and throw on some jeans?" she calmly suggests.

"I was going to do that, but it turns out my MOM, ugh, liked my bandana so much she bought one and is going to wear it the same way I do!" I say with impatience.

"OMG! NO!" she exclaims.

"YES!!" I retort.

"You are going to burn them, right?" she so dumbly asks.

"No I was going to wear them." I say sarcastically.

"We have a major crisis!" she cries.

"That's what I've been trying to tell you!" I almost yell.

"You have to do something!!!!" she screams.

"Obviously! Remember how I was teased and harassed last year because of my clothes?" I whimper.

"How could I forget," she answers.

"I can NOT have another year like that!! My outfit is crucial!" I explode.

"Your right," she agrees, "we have a lot of work to do; let's get started. If your year is like last year it won't be pretty, but if it is, we can at least be prepared."

It has been decreed (by Alana and I), for the first day of school I shall wear a white v-neck t-shirt with jeans. Of course, I will accessorize with bracelets and a pair of Converse Shoes. I don't want to wear something too crazy; wouldn't want to scare people away on the first day. I'm really nervous! What if no one likes me or thinks I'm even more of a weirdo than they did last year!!! My stomach is churning and making sounds, it's not really a pleasant feeling. It's almost like butterflies, except it isn't good excitement. It's like when your bones feel all tingly and your brain is in a rush, jumping from one thing to another in confusion. I think my outfit is going to look good, but who knows what other people will say. What if everyone makes fun of me? I don't deserve to be teased, but who does? It doesn't matter because I DO NOT care what other people think about me, yet, I do care what people think. I don't want to care, but sometimes I do. I must remember, all I can do is be myself and do my best. Diary, I'll fill you in on what happens the first day tomorrow night, wish me luck!

a dorie doodle

Dorie

xoxo

DORIE'S TWO CENTS *FOR SURVIVING NERVOUSNESS*

It's normal to be nervous before an event or when confronted with a new situation, especially on the first day of school. Many times when I have butterflies in my stomach, whatever I'm nervous or excited about turns out well. That is not to say, when I don't have butterflies, things don't turn out well either. When you are nervous don't dwell on the worst possible outcome, but think about the best possible outcome. As my mother *it's* always says, "positive thinking brings positive results." *true*.

Also, when I am nervous about something, I tend to beat myself up about trivial things such as, my legs are too big; by butt is too small; my face is full of zits; I need to shed some pounds; I'm not talented enough; or I'm not smart enough. Insecurities tend to be exaggerated with stress and anxiety. *read →* It is normal to feel some anxiety about your body and abilities at times, but try to remember these thoughts are coming from you and not from other people. When you are feeling insecure, realize you are just fine the way you are and your friends have chosen you as a friend because they like you, just the way you are, imperfections and all. Also, standing out is sometimes better than always fitting in. We sometimes feel we need to look or act a certain way to impress people. The truth is, you can be the best-dressed girl in town or have the best grades in school, but if you have a nasty personality and ridicule others, people may not want to be your friend.

at least → Whenever you look in the mirror, try to find something good about yourself, instead of something bad. If you keep doing this, you will find yourself feeling a lot better about your image and more confident in your abilities. In addition, you will be a lot happier and others gravitate toward happy, confident people. You should never make fun of somebody because they look a certain way, dress in a particular manner or live differently than you do. We can't always help our weight, birthmarks, scars, lifestyle or other self perceived imperfections.

People need to accept and embrace each other's differences without judgment. Wouldn't it be awfully boring if the world were full of people exactly like you or me? How could we each be unique? It's good to be different. Many times, we strive to be like super thin celebrities or other people we see in the news. Want to know a secret? A good friend of mine (who happens to be a boy) once told me that he likes a girl with a good sense of humor and some meat on her bones. The key is confidence, not looks!

REMEMBER THIS!

We don't all have to be stick thin with perfect clothes and hair to have people like us. We don't have to be superstars at sports or have straight A's in school. Just be happy with yourself and others will pick up on your confidence. Relax and accept yourself, imperfections and all and celebrate your uniqueness. In the real world, it's what's inside each person that *be unique* matters, not what we see on the outside!!!!

EXTRA REMEMBER THIS
(I DON'T HAND THESE OUT EVERYDAY)!

When you are feeling anxious, nervous or upset about something and are having trouble calming yourself, follow this technique (guaranteed to work most of the time).

really helpful

Three easy calming techniques for stressful situations:

1. As difficult as it may be, remove all negative thoughts from your mind and think of something positive. I think of music or do math problems in my head to distract me. Try any distracting and positive thought which works best for you.

2. If you are able to, do step one above sitting down with your eyes closed. If not, it is all right.

3. Start breathing slowly and deeply. Concentrate on your breathing; in and out; in and out.

a tad
bit .

This may seem really goofy, but give it a try. If you're busy concentrating on breathing, your troubles may disappear because you relax and your mind is free of stressful thoughts.

It's OK to be !
goofy !
fun

CHAPTER 2
NEW FACES,
BUT ARE THEY NEW FRIENDS?

THE REAL DEAL

The most common form of bullying is verbal bullying; name-calling and rumor-spreading. It is also common to bully each other through shunning or leaving a child out on purpose. (HRSA)

YOUR TWO CENTS

Question 1: Have you ever been a new girl? If so, how were you treated? *check Dorie's two cents for more info.*
Response: "I'm an army brat so I moved all over the country. In some schools people were nice to me, but in others they were not. It all depends on how well I fit in with the other students."
Question 2: When you see other new girls, how do you treat them?
Response: "Sometimes I just ignore them. Why should I have to babysit them?"

Dear Diary,

It's the end of the day and I have finished all of my homework. In a few minutes I'll be snoring under my sheets, but first I thought I would write you a little something. After all, I think the first day of school DOES set the tone for the whole school year. You know me, Diary, ever the dramatic actress so I may start sounding like a storyteller. It's so much fun to make your life into a story! Don't be surprised if I start ranting and raving in the middle of something, because I do tend to occasionally lose my train of thought. Also Dear Diary, I am about to share my inner most thoughts on these pages so please, get ready for anything! Anyway, this is somewhat how my first day played out.

"Beep-beep, beep-beep, beep-beep," this is what I woke up to. Why are alarms so annoying? I guess it's the point of alarms,

right? I am already missing the quiet mornings of summer! Every morning when the alarm wakes me up, I'm still sleepy and can never find the clock to shut it off, so the beeping just annoys me more. To make matters worse, I am so nervous...just try and imagine dear Diary, a young teenager nervous for her first day of school. Here I am lying in bed with annoying beeping sounds swirling around in my head for the first time in a long time.

Should I get out of bed or sleep a few more minutes? I snuggle a little deeper into my bed with my stuffed monkey. Better not risk another crisis, with me who knows what could happen. I slide out of bed; put on my slippers; and go downstairs to grab a quick bite to eat of granola and blueberries. Diary, want to know a random fact of knowledge? If you eat a healthy breakfast you can maintain your weight better and you will become sick less

often. Who knew? After breakfast, I bolt to the bathroom. If Luna gets there before me all hope is lost. She takes forever in the bathroom, even longer than me and no one thought this fact was possible, not even my parents! Coming out of her bedroom my sister sees me nearing the bathroom, she makes a run for it, trying to arrive before me and I stick my tongue out as I snag the most sacred room in the house. I won the battle for today but the big question is who will win the war?

After I'm done showering, blow drying my hair and applying makeup I exit the sanctuary giving it up to Luna, my foe. She glares at me as I head toward my room and I just smile and wave. I love the sweet taste of victory! No time to dwell on my win, I still have to dress. I look at my clock and oh no, only ten minutes until the bus picks me up, if it's running late. Thank God I picked out my outfit last night. After successfully dressing myself in seven minutes (I watched every clock tick), a new record, I dash out of the house and the few feet to the bus stop. My comrades are already loading the bus which I call "the jungle on wheels." I call it the jungle on wheels because it really is like a jungle, very wild and out of control. Obstacles, animals, ordeals, adventure…it's really survival of the fittest. So far, I've been able to survive, but who knows what will happen at any given point in time. Every year presents new faces and new situations. I cross my fingers and hope that I don't have too many new obstacles, animals, ordeals and adventures to face. I like adventure, but not if it's going to be unpleasant!

I know my sister is going to be late for the bus, so I try to make some time for her by "stalling." I would want her to do the same for me. I wave at the bus driver who sees me and motions for me to hurry. "Oh no, Mister Bus Driver, I have no intention of doing

bus
animal

that," I say to myself as I casually stroll toward the annoyed bus driver sitting at the head of the massive jungle. I examine the bus and its jumping bean contents. I can't say that I personally enjoy riding the bus; it's usually loud, raucous and it can be difficult to find a place to sit. Also, it's really unnerving for me to walk down the bus aisle because it appears all the people in the seats have nothing better to do than stare blankly at you and whoever else is getting on the bus behind you. You can never tell what they are thinking and I always guess it must be the worst possible thing.

It's also hard for me to find a place to sit. Since I'm the last bus stop, the bus is usually full and some people don't like to make room for others. Not naming any names or anything, but it can be really disturbing. I look behind me and I see Luna leaving the house. I speed up a little more and hop on the bus. I smile at the bus driver; he gives me more of a grimace. Now, time to face the aisle and the Bus Crowd (this would be all the kids who ride the "jungle" and especially the ones who are not so nice to me). I walk past the staring faces. I wonder why their stares bother me so much; I wonder if there's something wrong; like do I have a rip in my pants or something worse. I hope not. I know I'm fine this time because I

checked my outfit over and over last night so there is no need to worry. I'm just overreacting, I guess. I look around for an open seat but there are none, and no one slides over to make room for me. Golly, I didn't think I'm that strange. Good thing I went for the tame outfit of t-shirt and jeans, although some people may disagree. This really is making me feel self-conscious. Is it my outfit or my new pink hair? Why won't people scoot over and let me sit down?

"Excuse me," I say politely, "I need a place to sit, and do you think I could sit here?" The girl I ask just glares at me wide eyed like I'm crazy. "Did I mention I love your backpack," I add. I've learned

that one can never go wrong

me looking for a seat

with flattery because it always makes the person feel good and they think you are trying to be nice...which, of course, you are. Moreover, they will be overwhelmed with the fact that a complete stranger is being nice and they have no time to react. The girl looks blankly at me and then gives out a loud sigh. You know sighs are supposed to sound like the person is tired, but the real intent is sometimes to show how annoyed they are with you. OK, I'll admit it; the bus is starting to irritate me now.

After a brief pause, she moves over signaling that I can sit. I wonder why she is so angry, it's not like I'm that weird? This girl simply needs an attitude adjustment. I must remember and keep telling myself...it's her, not me...it's her problem, not

mine. It's hard to remember this when someone is staring obviously at you, and you alone, and sighing very loudly to make it known to everyone within reach that you are not welcome.

"My name is Dorie, what's yours?" I say to her, trying to strike up a conversation. Maybe she just started the day a little crummy. I mean, it IS the first day of school and all... I bet she is a really nice person and if she is not, maybe she can be with some good old enthusiasm. Not everybody takes to the end of summer vacation with a positive attitude.

"Dana," she softly mutters. Maybe she is tired, I think and maybe I should ask her, but she definitely doesn't look

tired. She's very pretty with wavy brown hair that reaches the middle of her back and doesn't appear to be very tall. Next to my imposing build, she looks like she's younger than me. I shouldn't be intimidated by her attitude, but I don't think I'm going to ask her if she is tired since she doesn't seem very friendly.

"Nice meeting you," I say. "I love your shoes. Where did you buy them?" As I said before, in keeping with my ideas about flattery... you can never ever go wrong.

"Chanel," she mutters out of the side of her mouth.

"Wow! Whatever that is, it sounds cool," I say. I get the impression that Dana doesn't feel like talking today. Oh well, I think I might as well say hi to the girls in the seat next to me and see if that goes any better.

"Hi, I'm Dorie, what is your name?" I ask.

"I'm Luan and this is Suzy," answered one of the girls sitting in the seat directly across from me. They are both around the same height as Dana. Luan has bouncy dirty blonde hair which hangs just below her shoulders. I couldn't help but notice that her voice

comes across as being just a tad bit grating, but she probably can't help it and I realize that I shouldn't be judging her because of her gravelly voice. Suzy has straight brown hair that hits her shoulders. All three of the girls I'm sitting around are dressed like they came out of some fashion magazine; very stylish.

"Nice to meet you. Did you have a good summer?" I ask.

"Fine," they both say before turning back to giggle about something. I guess everybody is a little grumpy about socializing in the morning, but I don't blame them. Oh well, it takes all types of people to make the world go around. I can't believe I didn't know these girls before. I usually know everybody, but then again it IS easy to miss somebody. They could also be new, but probably not. I surmise this because these girls are not nice enough to be new. Usually, new girls are shy and nice because they don't want to make enemies before they make friends. Then again, everybody is different and has a different way of dealing with situations.

Shortly, we arrive at school and the bus is ready to unload. After the mad, almost pile up rush to get off, I follow the crowd and walk into the main hallway of Westbrook Public School. The town built a new school two years ago and it looks really good from the inside and outside. It has two floors and I think it is enormous!! There are so many wings I'm always afraid I'm going to become lost. The school is green and white; our school colors. I think I might have preferred a different color scheme, but it's better than the old school which was falling apart and was quite gross. We are really lucky to have such a nice new school. Even though our town is kind of small, there are enough kids to fill up each classroom. Our school is considered small compared to others, but I wouldn't want anything bigger; for me it would be very overwhelming! Also, I'm glad we have fewer students in our school, because I'm able to get to know people better. Even though our school is big, it's pretty easy to navigate if you have a map. And of course I do have a map! Alana, Cass and I made it because we kept getting lost and we were always late for class. Speaking of Alana and Cass, I see them across the corridor... there they are!

I'm walking towards the middle of the central hallway where most of the lockers are located. I can see Alana and Cass standing at the end of the hallway by our old lockers and they are surrounded by students chatting excitedly about their summer vacation and the new school year.

"Alana," I yell, ignoring the looks from my fellow classmates. She turns around and as I take a step towards her, I fall flat on my face. I promptly stand up, but how embarrassing. I can hear people laughing and I look around for who tripped me. I

me on the ground

hear some familiar snickering and see Dana standing with Luan and Suzy. Dana looks at me with false innocence and says, "Oops." I want to hide my face and run away, but I know that will make it worse. It will only draw more attention and give people more reasons to tease me.

"Ta dah," I say, trying to hide my embarrassment. "I am such a klutz," I say uncomfortably. Why did they have to trip me; we just met? I could have broken my nose with that fall, doesn't she even care or know what she did is wrong? Must be their way of saying nice to meet you; more like not nice to meet you! Well another school year off to a great start. Why even bother telling on her, the school never takes it seriously unless your bleeding, then they have to do something because their afraid the parents will get the police involved.

"What a dweeb." "I know she is so weird," I hear voices saying. I ignore them and look straight ahead being more careful where I place my feet. I can feel my face burning; I bet it's beet red and I hearing buzzing in my head like little bees. I'm dizzy from the embarrassment, but I'm quickly getting myself back together. I tell myself, "that's ok, just keep walking. Deep breaths. More deep breaths." This is a little technique I always use when I'm feeling stressed and it calms me. If I'm busy focusing on breathing, then my mind doesn't have time to worry about anything else.

Remember to breathe and exhale, too!!

"Hey," I say when I finally reach Alana. She looks lovely as usual with a headband wrapped around her forehead, a polo t-shirt, jeans and her favorite flat shoes.

"Wow, you took a big fall, but you don't look embarrassed. I would be mortified," she exclaims. I look at her and raise an eyebrow and even though I am still embarrassed from the fall, with a false bravado I explain.

"You must remember my good friend, when something embarrassing happens, just crack a joke and keep going like nothing has happened and take deep breaths until you feel calm. If you act as if it doesn't matter, others will too. Don't ever cower or cry; it gives people a reason to tease you," I comment in one long rush.

"You should write that one down; it's a good one," Alana exclaims.

"You think?" I ask.

"Ya," she answers.

"Maybe I will add it to my Totally Notably," I inform her. If she saw how red my face was after the fall, then she would have known I had difficulty following this rule, especially because people were actually laughing at me and making sure I could hear their not so pleasant comments.

Note: add to Totally Notably

Now Diary, I haven't told you about my Totally Notably yet, so I had better explain. In you Diary, I vent about my day and give the 411, but in the Totally Notably, I am constantly noting information which is helpful to me and important enough to share with others. It is sort of like a portable notebook and I record information I want to be sure to remember. I include things like friend's phone numbers and birthdays or books I may have borrowed and need to return. I even jot down names of songs I like and want to download on my iPod. Sometimes when I'm bored, I even just sit and doodle in it to pass the time.

My Totally Notably contains all kinds of information and it is a handy resource to have when I need to remember something important and I'm afraid I will forget. Some of the notes are silly, but often this notebook is the ultimate survival guide and it resides right inside my locker. Anyone, including my friends, can add something to my Totally Notably if what they con-  tribute isn't mean or mean spirited. When they write in the Totally Notably, I remind them to be nice and no gossip because bad gossip results in bad feelings. Also, sometimes my Totally Notably contains what I've observed about various situations and problems in school. In my descriptions I don't express my personal opinions or feelings and NOT writing how I truly feel takes a lot of restraint! I don't want people to form their personal opinions based on MY personal opinions. As an example, I personally feel we

Lunch at School

should have more nutritional food at school. I know the cooks do a great job with the budget they have, but it sure would be nice to have tasty and healthy food. Also, I'm tired of eating food I can't identify and how can we concentrate in class if our stomachs are growling! I decided to note this idea in my Totally Notably so I can bring it up with the administration and I'm sort of keeping a daily food log to document my case. So you see Diary, this notebook records many different ideas from simple things like phone numbers to large ideas for change at school. I like to keep it available because some new tidbit of information is always popping up. Well Diary, now you know all about the Totally Notably and I have to admit, I don't know how I would survive without you both! Now where was I, Diary? Oh yes, back to my day and my story.

After I fell and before Alana and I could continue our fascinating conversation, the bell rang and we rushed to homeroom.

After homeroom, I had study hall in the library. When I reached the library, I saw a lot of familiar faces from last year. Alana and Cass were sitting at a table in the back closed in by book cases on either side; I joined them. Cass was clearly sleeping, but Alana looked wide-awake.

"Hey, looks like we have study hall together," I say.

"O, drat," Alana jokes.

"I met some new people on the bus and they are the ones who tripped me," I inform her.

"It seems like you're always meeting new people. What were they like? Do I even have to ask that question?" she asks.

"Well, I think they weren't feeling so excited about coming back to school; I'll put it that way," I remark.

"I.e. they weren't nice. I think I could see that," Alana smartly replies.

"We don't know that, look at you when you wake up early in the morning," I say with a smirk.

"Very funny! Being grumpy in the morning still wouldn't give them liberty to trip you," she reminds me.

We would have continued talking if the librarian hadn't shushed us. Her shushing only worked for a few moments and we continued to chat, but this time in lower voices. I looked around the library to make sure the librarian wasn't near so we could keep talking. I would have gone back to our conversation, but something stopped me. In the entryway to the library, there were two girls standing and looking really uncomfortable. They kept looking around for a place to sit, except I think they were too overwhelmed to know where to start. They must be new I thought.

"Look over there," I say to Alana.

"What, it looks like some newbies," she says with boredom.

"I think I'm going to invite them to sit with us," I comment with enthusiasm.

"Why?" she asks.

"Don't be such a meany! I'll be back in a minute," I retort. And with that, I'm off to meet some potential new friends.

meany

bo-beany

I reach the door about two seconds later and both girls look relieved to see me, while everyone else is just staring at their discomfort. Talk about rude!! Nobody likes being stared at when they know the people, but never mind when strangers are staring. If it was me, I would be feeling really insecure and wondering why people were staring; was it my outfit, was it my hair? Why do people find the need to make others feel uncomfortable? Don't they understand it's really hard to be a new girl!! Everyone has been new at something.

"Hey," I whisper, "I'm Dorie, what's your name?"

"I'm Ash," says one. She sounds nervous.

"I'm Nancy," says the other.She also sounds nervous.

I invite them to sit at our table and they follow. Nancy is quite small, a lot smaller than I am and she's pretty with brown hair falling to her shoulders which compliments her lovely green eyes. Ash is almost as tall as I am and this makes me glad! She wears her hair of brown ringlets just above her shoulders. After we sit down, I introduce them to Alana, who doesn't seem so thrilled they are sitting with us. Whatever, she'll just have to deal with the situation. Both girls seem really shy. I don't blame them; after all, they are new.

"So, where did you guys live before you moved here?" I ask.

"I lived in Maine," says Nancy.

"I lived in Rhode Island," says Ash.

"Very cool; from different states," I respond, "It must be hard to move to a different state, away from all of your friends," I say and decide I am going to be extra nice to them.

"If you want we can show you around the school so you get the gist of things," I say.

Nancy smiles and Ash thanks me. Looks like I've made two new friends. I believe Alana is sulking so I throw her a nasty look, and she stares back trying to look innocent. She is so funny, yet complicated! Sometimes Alana isn't the best at meeting new people, but once you get to know her, she is a blast.

43

chat,
bla'
blah,
blah
Shh
+
shh
:
S
i
l
e
n
c
e

The four of us chat until the librarian comes over and threatens to give us a detention, which none of us wanted on the first day. After that, nothing eventful really happened at school from a social point of view. Cass eventually woke up and welcomed the new girls to our group. I had lunch, some more classes, came home, had dinner and did homework. It was kind of boring. It's getting quite late so I'll pick this up later. Diary, thanks for listening to my day!

Dorie

XXOO XOOO   ♡

XOXO

DORIE'S TWO CENTS *FOR SURVIVING BEING THE NEW GIRL*

At some point in time, everybody has been the new person, maybe for a team, in a rehearsal, in a new school, or even for a meeting. Everyone has felt the anxiety one feels when they walk into a room and recognize not one person in the crowd. Often, you could start to sweat or fidget and I have yet to meet a person who enjoys this sensation. It doesn't matter the size of the group, there could be 2 people or 300 people, and you could still experience a tremendous amount of anxiety. When you are in a new situation, try following a few of these suggestions to reduce your anxiety and calm your nerves. Keep in mind, your results may vary depending on your personal situation and personality.

NEW GIRL SUGGESTIONS: → go to beginning of chapter to hear what others had to say

1. Before you enter the room, building or situation where you are going to be new, give yourself a pep talk. This may sound silly, but it

works! Point out all of your great qualities the new people will like. It will boost your confidence and people are attracted to confidence.

2. Walk into the area and survey your surroundings. Some people like to be surrounded by people; if this is you, walk to a large group of people and introduce yourself. Say it with a confident voice (you know what your name is) and a firm handshake. Always look people straight in the eye and smile because this will radiate your confidence and friendliness. If you are not comfortable with a large group, find a smaller, or perhaps the smallest group of people (even if it's just one person) and introduce yourself in the same fashion stated above.

3. Start a conversation; any pleasant subject will work. You could say something like, "I'm new here. Do you think you could explain ___?" In the blank insert any question you may have regarding the new environment or situation you may be experiencing. You can change the sentence to fit your needs. Also, asking for someone's advice will make them feel important and everybody likes to feel important. Another way to start a conversation is to compliment the person, whether it be on their soccer skills, cute shoes, or awesome clothes, because when you compliment someone, they feel good about themselves and think you're a nice person. Also, you can start a great conversation with a compliment. Look at the example below.

Example:

You: "You have a great aim when kicking the soccer ball."
Her: "Thanks. I started playing when I was eight." (The person may tell you a story and you should ask questions and seem genuinely interested. This may result in a great conversation from both parties.)
You: (if you want to become a better friend) "Maybe you could give me a few tips and show me a few moves."

just·t give it a try·

Her: "Definitely."

You may say to yourself, "that example would never work for me," but I am living proof it can happen. If you don't believe me, try it for yourself before dismissing the idea.

4. If you don't feel comfortable with the person you originally started talking with, you can always move to another group. Just excuse yourself politely (you don't want to make an enemy) and repeat the process with someone else. Keep practicing and it will become easier before you know it.

very true

REMEMBER THIS!

If you want to make new friends, you can't be afraid to approach people. If you just wait for someone to approach you, important opportunities to make friends may be missed. Just be confident and friendly. Also, remember to compliment people and before you know it, you will have new friends. I know you can do it!! If your still nervous, review the calming techniques from *Chapter 1* in *Remember This* for added confidence!

*Have no fear,
Dories (my) help
is HERE !*

CHAPTER 3
FRENEMIES, ENEMIES, AND MUCH MORE!

THE REAL DEAL

This needs to change!

Children are often bullied because of differences between them and others, whether because of appearance, intellect, or increasingly, ethnic or religious affiliation and sexual orientation. (NCPC)

YOUR TWO CENTS

Question 1: Do you belong to a clique? If so, why are you in that clique?

Response 1: "I belong to a group of close friends, but I wouldn't consider it a clique."

Response 2: "Yes, because we have the same interests."

Question 2: Do you consider cliques a good thing? Why or why not?

Response 1: "I don't because when you hang out with one person too much, you can get annoyed and fed up with them. I think it is good to have a variety of friends."

Response 2: "Sometimes, because some people in cliques are nice and others are not."

Dear Diary,

Today Ash and Nancy wanted to know about the cliques in our school, so I thought about how I would feel if I were new to the school and what I would need to survive. I agreed to give them a piece of my Totally Notably to help. I explained I have tips for every teacher, situation, person, place and thing and how I would be lost without my Totally Notably!

I also explained to Ash and Nancy how my Totally Notably contains what I've observed about the various groups, or the cliques, in my school. I encouraged them to form their own personal opinions and not adopt MY personal opinions. They should only know the facts, but judge for themselves. I agreed to give them the book first thing tomorrow.

quickly clique-y clique-y tip-y

So Diary, let me give you some information about cliques from the Totally Notably before I lend it to Ash and Nancy. I will give you the whole story, not the edited version in the Totally Notably, this way you can truly understand what a challenge school can be for me on a daily basis. Remember Diary, I leave the Totally Notably in my locker, anyone can see it! Only you know my true thoughts and feeling. If I can't tell you, who can I tell? Anyway, these are my observations and personal advice for navigating school! You know, it took me years of observing people and it hasn't all been fun!

THE DRAMA CLUB CLIQUE

The dramas are a clique led by Stella the Star. She is indeed a star because she stars in all of the school plays. However, sometimes she can cause trouble when she creates drama off the stage. Stella can be considered a frenemy. Diary, a "frenemy" is someone who can be a friend or an enemy, depending on the circumstances. Stella enjoys the attention she receives from gossiping about other people. And boy does she gossip! FYI: she shares this gossip with everybody. Her followers have been nick-named the "D Club" by us (us meaning, Alana, Cass and I). It is such a coincidence that Stella's entire clique has names which start with a "D"; even more coincidental is drama starts with a "D!" What word could describe this clique better than drama? Hence the name, the Drama Club.

Duh guys, it's the duh-club.- did I say d'uh? I meant d-club

Stella + the D-Club

How To Get Along With The Drama Club: 1. Ask about the latest gossip or drama, but don't get involved. 2. Compliment their outfits. 3. Discuss their latest roles in the plays. 4. Remember to talk about them a lot; they like it because it makes them feel more important.

THE POPULARS CLIQUE

In my school, The Populars aren't rightfully named because they are popular by dictionary definition (nice to everybody and well liked). One of the only reasons why they are popular is because almost everybody is afraid to stand up to them!! People are afraid of The Populars because they are often really cruel, and for some unknown reason, people believe their malicious gossip! One of my close friends says that at his school, his friends would brand our schools "The Populars" as "The Snobs" and the nice and well liked people are the most "popular" in the school. Why my school has to be backwards, I have no idea. All I know is if people in my school would try a group correction, I am 99% sure we would have the same definition for "populars" and "snobs" as my friend's school, but I haven't been able to muster up a group to work on this.

Oooo, look at me, I'm so popular NOT

Oh Diary, I need to explain "group correction." This is when a group (meaning more than one person) confronts a person in a calm manner about some undesirable action or problem which may have occurred. If a group discusses and expresses concern regarding this person's unacceptable behavior, the person may listen, make changes and possibly make amends. Group correction is always used in a calm and positive way to bring positive results and it is very effective in many situations. It basically is standing up for yourself or others in a mature way and caring about both sides of the story.

Anyway, back to the story. The ringmaster of The Populars in my school is Carry. Many worship her, while others refer to her as a tyrant (more commonly known with Alana and me as "evil dictator"). One must beware not to be on this group's bad side for it could

M = Moody = meany

result in negative consequences (this has been gained from personal experience). To avoid trouble with The Populars, make sure you constantly compliment them and keep them talking about themselves, just like the approach one takes with the Drama Club. Not only is it the best way to make friends, but they will be so busy talking about themselves, they won't have time to talk about you! If you ever need anything from The Populars, always contact Sally over Carry since she is more willing to reach out to people and be helpful. Carry and Sally are best friends, but they don't always see eye to eye. It is my personal belief that if Sally was in charge of The Populars, there would be no need to call anybody an "evil dictator." Sally is actually a REAL popular person because she is nice. This is the way it should be and the way "popular" is defined at my friend's school. I think Sally just got swept up in a clique full of meanies. Sally seems to follow the leader, Carry, without objecting. At times, you can see she doesn't like what is going on, but she doesn't say anything. It is my personal belief she doesn't want to be kicked out of The Populars, so she holds her tongue and says nothing.

NOTE: For the best results, steer clear of this group entirely. Also, if they make up rumors about you, just ignore it, because by tomorrow, it will be yesterday's news. There will be new gossip to replace the gossip about you.

EXTRA NOTE: Group correction doesn't work well with a group of two people, it is best to call in more reinforcements.

EXTRA, EXTRA NOTE: Don't ditch people to try hang out with The Populars, otherwise if this group starts hating you again, you

will be left completely friendless. Most people would all like to look as good; have as many frenemies/friends; play sports equally as well; or get the good grades of some of The Populars, however, we all need to remember that true popularity in life is based on self-confidence, kindness, and making OTHERS feel good about themselves. Listening to and having compassion for others, draws people to you like a magnet. Having these qualities will make you naturally a real popular person by dictionary definition. Respecting yourself and others is the answer to real friendships.

ALMOST POPULAR CLIQUE

they look exactly like the populars

This group is under the impression they are extremely popular, when they really don't have much of an impact on the social scene. This is because most of their actions model that of The Populars, so people pay little notice to them. If someone wants some good gossip or wants to be more popular, they would rather go to the head honcho (The Populars) than second in command (Almost Populars). This clique is almost entirely made up of people younger in years than The Populars, and they will most likely take the place of The Populars when the people in that group move on or graduate. Some members of the Almost Popular migrate between their group and The Populars or Wanna Be Populars so these people usually have friends and frenemies in all three groups.

HOW TO: to be safe, completely avoid them. Make no extra effort to socialize. Always be polite, but no more, because you could be the target of gossip.

WANNA BE POPULAR CLIQUE

p + wP = weirdo

Members of this clique tend to try to be like The Populars and they will do anything to impress The Populars to become a part of their exclusive group. They dress, talk, act, etc., exactly like The Populars. The members of the Wanna Be Popular are generally nice people, unless in the company of The Populars. When they are with The Populars, they will try to show off and you could be

51

the butt of their jokes. I don't think they realize some of The Populars really don't want
them to become part of The Populars. One
must remember, if you are looking for a last-
ing friendship, the Wanna Be Popular Clique may not be the first
place to look because they can be fickle and change their behavior
and opinions quite quickly.

NOTE: If The Populars have made it clear they like you, this
clique will treat you like a hero. Be warned, this WILL NOT last
because The Populars change their minds daily. Try not to feel hurt
by this group's actions and enjoy them on their good days.

EXTRA NOTE: If you join this clique, you may be pressured
to do things you don't want to do to impress The Populars. I have
heard, but can't confirm this may include, but is not limited to,
hazing, bullying, cheating, stealing, and lying to people you care
about, and possibly even consuming drugs and alcohol. If your
friends pressure you to do something, even though you make it
clear you don't want to, then they are not your real friends. Move
on and find new friends.

no picture for they also look exactly like the populars

NADAS CLIQUE

There is not much information concerning this clique because
being in close proximity can be dangerous to your health. They are
called the Nadas because they have some serious problems with
food and eat close to nothing; zip, zap, nada. One reason it can be
dangerous to be near them is because their bad eating habits or fear
of eating, may rub off on you. When you are with them, you may
begin to feel bad about your weight and body image and start dieting. The Nadas need to learn to be happy with the body
they have. Everybody is different and this is what makes
each of us special. Wouldn't it be boring if the world was
made up of millions of YOU or millions of ME? I wouldn't
want everyone I know to be just like me because then I

wouldn't be original. In fact, nobody would be original if we were all alike.

DANGER: If you pay attention to what these people say, you may possibly become anorexic, bulimic, look like a skeleton or die from the complications of starvation.

NOTE: If a close friend starts making fun of your weight, tell them to stop! It is not nice to make fun of someone because of their body size!! Plus, most people make fun of someone else because they are insecure about something within themselves. Making fun of someone is their immature and insecure way to assure themselves they are fine.

EXTRA NOTE: Be nice to these people because they have feelings just like you and me. Also, make sure  you don't label someone as a Nada, just because they are skinny. Bodies come in all shapes and sizes and some people are genetically thin or need to avoid complete food groups because they have allergies.

LOWER PARKING LOT CROWD CLIQUE

At our school, there are two parking lots for students who drive; one by the gym, and the other down the hill and away from the first parking lot and gym: we call this "the lower parking lot." The Lower Parking Lot Crowd has gained its name because it spends the majority of its time in the lower parking lot (I always wonder how they get away with it; don't they have classes?). You can sometimes spot a member of this group by the way they dress; more gothic or emo with piercings and tattoos, which are supposed to be hidden, but are in plain view (although I think some just dress this way to be different). The Lower Parking Lot Crowd breaks rules because they say they were born to be rebellious. They sometime have a strange smoke smell, not sure what it is, but I have heard the gossip. What they do in the lower parking lot is a mystery, but I personally have seen people smoking cigarettes. Alana and I are not sure, but we believe that some of

the so-called "cigarettes" are drugs. We cannot confirm, so we keep this information to ourselves and do not spread rumors.

There have been rumors that some members are no longer "so innocent." On account of the fact there is no physical evidence (obviously) except gossip, we remain confident the rumors are not true, or at least we hope so. Our minds do wonder, but it wouldn't be polite to ask such a question (although Alana disagrees). Alana loves to say, "We should be up front and not afraid of asking questions. If you believe gossip, you are a fool. If you do not ask questions, you are a bigger fool." We will leave Alana to her opinions and me to my opinions.

I personally have a friend from grade school who belongs to The Lower Parking Lot Crowd. Even though we have grown apart, we sometimes talk in the hallways. She comes from a tough family with problems most kids have never experienced, and she is forced to babysit her six siblings while her parents work. She is trying to look cool/tough so she is not made fun of for living the way she does. She doesn't do all the things The Lower Parking Lot Crowd is rumored to do, but she uses their reputation as protection so no one gossips about her or her family.

DANGER: This is a fast crowd in unknown territory. AVOID, AVOID at all costs!!!!!!

NOTE: Do not be cruel to these people. We don't know their life story so show some empathy!

SMARTY PANTS CLIQUE

These are the techies of tomorrow. Some people call them The Geek Department, but that would infer that all of them wear high-waisted pants and pocket protectors with calculators and pens, which they don't. Just about every person in this clique is nice. The only mean people are those who stick their noses up at you because you don't have straight A+'s. Unfortunately, the people in this clique are teased the most, which is not nice. I always stand up for them, but sometimes they don't even stand up for themselves and this drives me crazy! Many of these people are so nice, they let people walk all over them and this is not right! Sometimes I wonder if they know something I don't know. Their confidence seems to be unshakable, and I wish I could be in on their secret to this confidence.

keep
a
walking

NOTE: Always stand up for yourself in a non-violent or non-abusive way. All you have to do is say, "stop, I don't like that," and walk away. It works even better when you have a group of people saying "stop" to a bully, because the bully is then more likely to stop the abusive behavior. FYI: that's called group correction and in case you missed it, here's a quick Dorie reminder of "group correction"; when a group of people nicely tell a person what they are doing is not right. Always remember, power is in numbers!

SPORTYS CLIQUE

These people are the leaders of all of the sports teams, the best of the best in sports. They are just as popular as The Populars, except they can be a lot nicer because they often have better self-esteem because of their abilities on the playing field. I have heard they sometimes hold wild parties. I really don't know, since I have never been invited, but I imagine the parties can be dangerous based on the school gos-

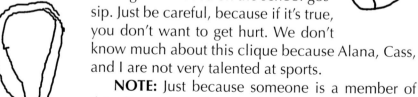

sip. Just be careful, because if it's true, you don't want to get hurt. We don't know much about this clique because Alana, Cass, and I are not very talented at sports.

NOTE: Just because someone is a member of this clique, doesn't mean they enjoy or attend wild parties. They could just enjoy sports and hanging out with their teammates. Also, gossip is, well, how I should say this, gossip!

UBER DUBERS CLIQUE

Uber Dubers are really anybody who doesn't fit into a clique. Some may call us outcasts, but it is really nice to not be categorized because we like not being labeled. This is where Alana, Cass and I belong. Anyone can hang out with us, unless you are mean and judgmental. We always try to be polite, even when it's hard to be nice. We are the group your parents might call "popular," but in our school we are labeled "a bit different." Popular really means generally liked and polite to all people (which we are). We try not to judge others and do our best to accept everybody for who he or she is. Unfortunately, we are teased and made fun of because of our easy going outlook. We have the confidence to be ourselves, even if others don't approve. I have to admit Diary, this is the best way to enjoy life.

NOTE: We can often be seen hanging out with different groups; we don't just stick to our immediate peer group.

ARTSY CLIQUE

People in the artsy clique are generally very talented in a variety of performing and visual arts. This group includes students from band, orchestra, choir, photography and theatre. I find them to be very pleasant, kind and extremely interesting. Unfortunately, sometimes they are made fun of by The Populars (I think it's because The Populars are jealous of their undeniable confidence).

NOTE: If you wish to be friends with such people all you have to do is be nice (and possibly a bit creative).

FLOATERS

Floaters aren't a clique; they are people who don't belong to one particular clique. Floaters are people who have friends in many different cliques and hang out with a variety of people; therefore, it would be very difficult to classify them into one particular group because they have such a large variety of friends and interests. Someone who is a Floater may be involved with cheerleading, the soccer team, the choir and even the photography club. They have friends from all of the cliques because of all of their activities. Many of the students in my school are Floaters and it's pretty cool. If I weren't in the Uber Dubers Clique, I would be a Floater. I guess I kind of am a Floater though, because I often hang out with friends in different groups, but I have been hanging out with Alana and Cass for so long, I'm sort of grouped with the Uber Dubers. Hope Ash and Nancy find this information from my Totally Notably helpful (although Diary, you know the truth and the whole truth)!!

Dorie

Dear Diary,

Nancy and Ash liked my Totally Notably and think it's really helpful. If I was new, I would like to have an experienced friend with a guidepost to navigating the social mine field at my school. I've been having trouble getting accustomed to being back at school, but once I settle down, I know I'll be just fine. I must remember, every year is an adjustment and it takes time to settle into a new grade!

Dorie

Hurray!

DORIE'S TWO CENTS *FOR SURVIVING JUDGMENTS*

It's normal to judge people because it's human nature, but sometimes we need to step back and look at why we are making judgments. Do we judge people because they are different from us, and is it fair to form an opinion about someone based on their appearance, mannerisms or peer group? Do you want to be judged, possibly misunderstood, and placed in one specific clique? People are complex and therefore have many different sides to their personalities. We often can't see the complexities, but if you actually take the time to explore someone's personality, you may find a completely different person than you expected.

Judging isn't exactly fair to the person being judged and often you are wrong in your assessment of their personality. You could easily make the mistake of interpreting someone's shyness for rudeness because they won't socialize. Also, you could incorrectly assume someone who dresses in black is gothic and possibly dangerous or someone who dresses in pink with blonde hair is dumb. These are incorrect stereotypes and we all have made inappropriate judgments. If we want to understand people better and make new friends, we often have to ignore our initial feelings about a person and really look closely at their true personality. People are complex and you need to take your time before forming opinions!

Every school has groups or cliques and we often judge them based on gossip or our personal opinions. Just because a person belongs to a clique, doesn't mean they always identify with the ideas of the clique. As an example, in my school some people who are part of The Populars are extremely nice, but they are shy and afraid to stand up to the group. They don't like the teasing, but are afraid if they say anything then they may become tomorrow's gossip. Their silence may not be right, but they may be too afraid to comment. Try to keep an open mind and really get to know someone before forming opinions. Also, concerning the Nadas Clique, if you or someone you know has serious issues with food and you are wor-

we are unique

ried they have an eating disorder please, see my *Eating Disorder Fact Sheet* at the end of this book. It will be very helpful!

REMEMBER THIS!

← Read!

It takes many different types of people to make the world go around and they are all here on our earth. You don't have to like everyone, but try to be as accepting and respectful as possible. We all will have our differences, enjoy and respect them. Don't try to change someone, instead appreciate each person's uniqueness. Also, always remember to be true to yourself, and agree to disagree with others. Tolerance brings acceptance!

If you tolerate, then you ate the hate!

CHAPTER 4
THE BUS JUNGLE: THAT INCLUDES
THE NOT SO INNOCENT BYSTANDERS.

THE REAL DEAL

Bullying often involves groups of students picking on another student and there is often a "ring leader." Many students do not take action to stop the bullying because they are afraid of being bullied themselves, because they want to be part of a popular group, or because they simply are not sure how to help. (HRSA) *check Bullying Fact Sheet at back of book for ways to help*

YOUR TWO CENTS

Question 1: If you saw the "cool" people bullying someone, would you speak up even though if you did, you could be their next target?
Response: 90% of people who answered this question said "Yes." Let us try and keep it that way.
Question 2: Why have you kept silent when you saw someone being bullied?
Response 1: "I was terrified I would be the next target."
Response 2: "I didn't think it was my business to get involved."

Dear Diary,

It is a fact; my bus ride is now unacceptable because the bullying is out of control. At first, I thought many people were not morning people so I gave them the benefit of the doubt. I thought the morning hours just made them grumpy, but that's not the case. I've tried to excuse their behavior

and forget, but the only way to say it is, they simply "ARE NOT NICE!" I really do not know what to do, I am very confused!

Dorie

BUS CROWD BULLIES

Dear Diary,

I decided the first course of action would be to decide what exactly I think people are doing to hurt my feelings, make me anxious or annoyed and to note this in you Dear Diary. After I write down the problem, I may think of things to make the situation better or resolve the problem, and then I will test it out. This is a start and we'll see what happens. Tomorrow I'll start making my notes. Diary, you need to stay home. I can't take you out of my bedroom, so I'm going to take some general notes at school and when I'm finished, I will write everything that's important in you.

Dorie

Dear Diary,

Here is what I noted today at school. Diary, you get the full version with all my opinions! This is about some of the people from the Bus Crowd and what they do to tick me off.

Luan: She is a grade below me and is part of the Almost Popular Clique. On my bus, she is considered somewhat annoying, yet she is generally accepted by everybody.

What ticks me off: she makes fun of me while we're on the bus. I'm busy studying and she tells me I'm not smart or other rude comments and she makes loud noises so I can't concentrate. On numerous occasions I've told her to stop, but it doesn't work. The only thing that works is sitting on the opposite end of the bus, but sometimes I'm not able to do this.

Suzy: She is a genius and I have heard she gets straight A's. People don't mind her because she doesn't make much of a ruckus.

SUZY

What ticks me off: when someone is making fun of me she will add really snappy insulting comments that other people work off. It really hurts my feelings because I'm not stupid or a slut (her most commonly used insults) and I don't antagonize her. Sometimes I want to yell at her and say "What are you doing, why are you bugging me? What have I done to you to make you do this to me?"

Dana: She is the ring leader of the Almost Populars and can bridge into The Populars. Many at school consider her cruel, but on our bus she is worshiped. She uses common Populars bullying tactics such as; making people feel insecure about their bodies; picking on

everything about a person until the victim wants to burst into tears. She also spreads malicious gossip and uses her power of gossip spreading as a threat. The reason some people worship her is because they want to be like her so they can join her clique. They may also be wary of what she would do if they didn't worship her because they could become the target of her gossip.

Queen
of the
meanies

What ticks me off: she picks on me all the time as if she has nothing better to do. My mother always taught me not to lower myself to her playing level because then I will be just like her – a bully. I try to be the better person.

Unfortunately, because of this I am picked on. It's hard to be the better person and say nothing. I don't really like to always be nice, but I know it's the right thing to do. Telling her to stop or moving away from her doesn't work and it actually makes the prob-

Note: if I'm telling someone; clearly it's past the point of ignoring!

lem worse. If I talk to the school, they just tell me to deal with it and nothing changes. They say I need to quit being "so sensitive" and "try to work it out." I'm not being sensitive and how can I work it out when she won't stop saying mean things about me? When she starts her teasing, everyone else joins in and I don't think I can deal with much more of it.

Mark: He needs two seats on the bus; one for himself and one for his ego. That may sound a tad bit mean, but it's so true. He is a local hero with all of his guy friends and is part of the Almost Populars.

What ticks me off: he, Dana, and Wayne (Diary, I'll explain him next) make fun of me a lot. It seems like there is no escaping. Sometimes I think he and Wayne do it to impress Dana; trying to make her laugh at my expense. Even when I sit on the opposite end of the bus, I can still hear them making fun of me. It's becoming really hard not to say anything back. He has had detentions in the past because of his remarks towards me, but it doesn't seem to be making any difference because he keeps doing it. The school doesn't seem to think it's a big deal so he continues. They tell you to "ignore it" and "don't respond and it will quit," but who can ignore it when it really hurts your feelings and why do they treat it so casually? I guess if they don't see it, then it isn't happening.

Wayne: He probably needs three seats on the bus. I personally think he is part of the Wanna be Popular Clique, but he kind of drifts between cliques with the name popular in it. He is good friends with some people in The Populars, but he isn't always allowed to hang out with them and I'm not sure why. I don't think I will ever comprehend the inner workings of The Populars.

What ticks me off: he takes mean to a new level because he actually kicks me. I tell him to stop, but he doesn't. Even with numerous detentions last year, he doesn't stop. The school doesn't really take it seriously, so he feels he can keep doing it. What if he

MAKE A STAND kicks me so hard someday that I break a bone or worse? Now the bullying becomes something real and I can call the police. Will they take it seriously then? Do I have to involve the police for them to say "Wayne, what you're doing is wrong and it needs to stop." I ALWAYS try to stay clear of Wayne, but sometimes I can't.

Joe: He is not as bad as the other people, but he is also not as well liked. It is hard to classify him because sometimes he becomes an outcast when he refuses to go along with cruel behavior.

me über scared

What ticks me off: he isn't really a mean guy, but he'll go along with whatever someone tells him to do, even if that person isn't nice to him. I want to yell at him and say, "You're too good for these people! Just be yourself and you'll be happier in the end."

(B)uthead! (U)ntame! (G)one! (L)unatic! (Y)ikes!

This is the list of people who irritate me on my bus every day; I call them the "Bus Crowd Bullies." Obviously, there are more people who ride the bus but the rest of the "Bus Crowd" doesn't bother me. I call them the "not so innocent bystanders," these are the people who see everything and do nothing to help. They are the witnesses to the bullying, yet when asked, pretend they saw nothing happen. They are "not so innocent bystanders" because they watch me being hurt and do nothing. When they do not take a stand and help defend me by saying stop to the bullies, then they are part of the problem of bullying and could also be called a bully. If I was seriously hurt and they just watched me being hit and kicked and did nothing to stop it, they could be called in as a witness. I'm really stumped because it's hard to ignore the Bus Crowd Bullies and telling on the bullies doesn't change things because the school doesn't take it seriously.

Even when my mom calls the school, nothing changes because they refuse to deal with the problem. My parents don't want to call the police for every kick, but they said if I am seriously hurt they sure will take action because then they can prove there is abuse. The hard part is it's the bullies' word against mine and it's sad to think someone has to show blood to prove their case. I don't understand why I can't feel safe in school because I know I have rights. For goodness sake, this is America and we have laws to keep us safe! What is wrong with my school and don't they care? Also, my parents can't drive me to school because they have to go to work and there isn't another bus that picks up in my area. I'm also not allowed to bike to school. I think I'm going to try to ignore them and sit as far away as possible (if I can).

If it doesn't work, I'll try talking to Ms. Nechman, my counselor. Maybe she has some ideas of how to stop the bus dilemma. I know I'm not alone and other people also have problems going to and from school, whether they take a bus or walk.

Dorie

DORIE'S TWO CENTS *ON SURVIVING AND NOT BEING A "NOT SO INNOCENT BYSTANDER"*

It is important you understand what bullying is before you accuse someone of being a bully. Bullying is anything that directly or indirectly hurts another person physically or emotionally. It is not limited to but includes; gossiping (any form), physical aggression, verbally attacking another person, and watching any of the above but not stopping it from happening. Also, under the laws of some states, if a school knows about the problem of bullying and someone is hurt, the school district is held liable. In the United States we have laws to protect us from being harassed and assaulted.

In the *Dorie's Two Cents* in *Chapter 5,* I explain the legal side of bullying and your rights in more detail, but for now I want to concentrate on the importance of the "not so innocent bystander." This form of bullying, watching but not stopping, is not commonly acknowledged

This is just as bad as bullying!

as a form of bullying. A "not so innocent bystander" watches or hears someone being bullied, but doesn't do or say anything to stop it. Often their excuses are "I didn't want to get involved," "let someone else help" or "there is nothing I could I have done to stop it."

When I was being bullied on the bus, many times I asked for help from bystanders who were quietly watching me being bullied. They all said, "I don't want to get involved." No one was asking them to get involved; I was only asking them to say stop to the Bus Crowd Bullies. There is power in numbers and it's called group correction. This is when you have a formidable group, (preferably more than two people), and you kindly, but firmly, tell the bully to stop. It works because the bully usually doesn't want to pick on a group, only a person.

Clearly, my fellow bus mates weren't aware of this. If I would have been seriously injured, everyone who watched and ignored the abuse would not be legally responsible for the assault and battery, but they could be questioned as a witness to the crime. Even if a state does not have anti-bullying laws, our government in the United States does

don't SKIP & show friends

offer legal protection. In the back of this book I have a **Bullying Fact Sheet** and please read it because it will help you understand the legal terms associated with bullying. It will also list the states which have passed anti-bullying laws so you can understand your rights.

You do not have to take being bullied so please speak up (tell an adult who can help) and quit suffering in silence. Also, please realize there have been many deaths due to bullying and many times the deaths could have been stopped if the "not so innocent bystanders" had gotten off the fence, taken a stand and helped. In fact, much of today's school violence is tracked back to being bullied.

REMEMBER THIS!

Next time you see somebody being bullied, don't just watch and hope you won't be the next victim!! Join with your friends and tell the bully to stop and go ask an adult for help. Become involved and help stop the problem of violence. Every child should feel safe and no one should ever live in fear. There is power in numbers and we need to gather together and stop all forms of bullying because our schools should be safe environments for us to learn! If your state doesn't have anti-bullying laws, get involved and contact your state representatives. Don't ever forget, we all need to be a part of the solution to end the violence of our world so let's join together and stop the violence of bullying in our schools!!!!

Be a Friend
End the hate
Spread the Love

CHAPTER 5
THE BUS BULLY CROWD STRIKES, AGAIN!

THE REAL DEAL

what would happen if we stopped following?

Surprisingly, bullies appear to have little difficulty in making friends. These friends are often followers that do not initiate bullying, but participate in it. (NYVPRC)

YOUR TWO CENTS

Question 1: Have you ever been bullied on the bus? Did your bus driver or another adult do anything to stop the bullying?
Response: "Yes, I have but the bus driver was too busy trying to keep everybody on the bus quiet that he just told me to ignore them. I don't think he realized it's hard to just ignore somebody who is harassing you!"
Question 2: Have you ever been bullied to the point you lost your temper?
Response: "Yes, I started yelling back when some girls were calling me names and laughing at me."

Dear Diary,

I couldn't do it. This time I couldn't just ignore the Bus Crowd Bullies. I tried sitting as far away as possible from Luan, Dana, Susie, Joe, Wayne and Mark, but I am the last stop on the bus route so very few seats were open. Definitely, this was a sign of a series of nasty events to soon follow. It is not a pleasant memory to relive, but I will bring it from the deepest pit of my mind so that you too, dear dairy, can feel my emotions. It went a little something like this.

my brain

When I stepped on the bus, I could tell it was not going to be pretty. Dana had a look to her eyes like she was in the mood for fun; i.e. harassing me. When I was nearing the only open seat, a foot flew out from a seat and sent me flying head first into the dirty ground of the bus floor. I couldn't believe Dana tripped me again and acted as if it's no big deal. It IS a big deal! Hello dumb Dana, it's called assault and battery and it's illegal!! I heard giggles with high fives and tried to contain my anger and tears while hot embarrassment burned my face. I stood up, brushed off my outfit now full of dirt, and sat down across from Dana and Mark. My arm was

this is how I imagined myself after the bus ride

hurting from the fall, so I placed my backpack on my lap. I faced straight ahead and told myself that it was only a ten minute ride to school, I could do it. I heard Dana and Mark exchange a few whispers and laughs with some "Dories" in between. I continued to ignore them because I knew they only wanted to get me going and see me upset, so I pretended not to see or hear them. With this approach it "may" stop I kept reminding myself. When I say "may" it's one of those things you put in finger quotes because looking back on it, you realize it was false hope, but worth a try. Anyway, before I knew it, Dana and Mark's whispers were becoming more and more audible. Finally, they decided to speak to me about whatever they found so hilarious.

whisper, whisper, dorie, whisper, giggle dorie, whisper, giggle, whisper

"So, Dorie, do you have a boyfriend or anything?" asked Dana in a slimy tone of voice. I ignored her; no way was I going to be pulled into anything. She repeated her question once again in a calmer tone someone cruel would use to hide a dreadful insult. Once again, I pretended to be engrossed in the history book conveniently in my backpack and ignored Dana's remarks.

"Dude, I don't think she's listening to you," said Mark to Dana.

At this Dana's face turned red; I think she was becoming upset and she reiterated her question once

me really scared

again in a more forceful tone. She looked at her cronies, the Bus Crowd Bullies, for backup, but they all shrugged.

I was internally overjoyed because I had finally made Dana stop by giving her the silent treatment. As I celebrated my victory a little too early, I didn't notice that Wayne was aware of my mood. I guess in his mind, I can't be happy if it makes Dana upset, so he decided to impress Dana and assert his power.

"Hey," he barked, "She's talking to you!" He followed his remark with a kick to my shin. I looked at him and then down at my history book. *Wayne is a big pain*

I will not succumb, I thought. He kicked me again and hit me on the head and arm with his textbook and it really hurt. I tried to ignore him, but I couldn't. I was angry no one on the bus or in school would help. They didn't take Wayne's hitting and kicking me seriously and say "Stop it Wayne!" At this point, something exploded inside me and I could no longer sit quietly and take his abuse; I was tired of being the bully target!

"Would you just knock it off!!!" I screamed at him. I continued to glare and felt such anger; I thought my eyes were burning in the back of my head and would soon pop out. He stopped and was actually surprised; I think others on the bus were too, because they turned around to see who was causing such a ruckus. The bus driver noticed the commotion and motioned for me to keep quiet and I nodded back to assure him I understood. I went back to my history book, trying to keep my fury inside so I didn't have another explosion, which at this point, seemed inevitable.

Bad Mad

The Bus Crowd Bullies were left dumfounded, but it only took a moment for Wayne to bounce back mad as a hornet. I was truly surprised when the person who told him to stop was none other than Dana.

"Just stop, it won't do any good," Dana said back to Wayne. You could tell it was difficult, but Wayne gradually regained his self-control and calmed down. "It doesn't matter anyway, we all know there is NO way Dorie could *ever* have a boyfriend. I mean, seriously, look at her, she's so ugly, who could possibly be attracted to that thing. She would probably have to pay someone to even kiss her," continued Dana in a sarcastic manner.

Yes, she did call me a "thing" and I did not take kindly to that one bit and something inside me snapped. Before she could even open her mouth, I unleashed all of my fury in a string of words I don't think I have ever used before. I felt as if I was pushed to the edge because I was kicked, hit and insulted one too many times. Looking back on the situation, I can see this was not the right approach to handle the problem, but I was so angry, hurt and confused I couldn't stop myself and see things clearly.

me + Dana's insult=

Kabbom

"Dana," I exploded, "Why don't you just shut your freaking trap right now!!" (I have never used the term freaking trap!) "You have no right to talk to me that way. By the way, just because you are the one who has to pay people to go out with you, doesn't mean you have to turn it around so it looks like I do!! I am so stinking sick of all of you obnoxious people making fun of me, hitting me, kicking me, and just being your plain good for nothing selves!!! Just because you aren't the prettiest, smartest or most talented people in the world, doesn't mean you can take out all of your stupid insecurities on me!!!!!! I have feelings and I am a person!! Clearly you don't have feelings, because your hearts are cold and cruel; black as coal and hard as stone!! I am so sick of you all!! Just leave me alone!!!! It's not my fault that you have nothing better to do with your lives than make fun of me!!! Find a new hobby or suffer the consequences!!!" I screamed so loud that by the time I had finished my little speech, everybody on the bus had turned in amazement.

The bus driver was now concerned and motioned for me to move to the front seat and the Bus Crowd was staring with their jaws hanging open. I had tears in my eyes, my hands were balled in fists, my body was shaking and my face was as red as fire. Even my ears burned as the blood pumped wildly through my body.

So over this!

As soon as I got home, I ran into the house crying with Luna hot on my heels. When I calmed down, I talked to my mom and she didn't take my explosion well and was quite surprised with my behavior, but she was more concerned with putting a stop to the bus harassment. Mom said she would talk to the school because clearly the situation had reached the point of assault and the bullying needed to be stopped. She was reluctant to immediately call the police because there was no physical evidence. She needed to talk with the school first and ask them to talk to the other students on the bus to confirm my story. Surely with this approach we could solve the problem and she needed the schools cooperation. Also, she was sure they would investigate because the problem was escalating and someone could be seriously hurt. The school would then have legal consequences and responsibilities. In the past they had refused to deal with the bullying, claiming the issues weren't serious, only normal childhood squabbles. The only thing she was worried about was that it could be difficult to prove the abuse without someone on the bus backing my story.

Mom

I explained the bus driver really had no idea because he only saw the commotion of me yelling and did not see the kicking or hitting. My only hope was the "not so innocent bystanders" because even if Luna explained, they would say she is prejudice to my side of the story. Mom was angry because she felt no child should ever feel in

I hate the bus!

danger on the bus or in school. Also, she would talk with the school and see if I could ride another bus. Mom also expressed she wished she could drive me to school and I know she does. I feel bad that SHE has to feel bad about this.

It's just not fair! Why do the Bus Crowd Bullies have to pick on me out of everybody on the whole bus? I don't understand. Why don't the other people on the bus stand up for me when they can clearly see I'm outnumbered? As I have previously mentioned, they are "not so innocent bystanders." Don't they know being a "not so innocent bystander" is a form of bullying!! They see what's going on and it makes me so mad they won't help me defend myself. I want to scream my head off, (which I did)!!!! I feel like there is so much more I want to tell the Bus Crowd Bullies, but I know it will make matters even worse. I will stay strong though and make sure the Bus Crowd Bullies don't affect me ever again.

Dorie

DORIE'S TWO CENTS *FOR SURVIVING BULLYING AND REALIZING THERE ARE LAWS TO PROTECT YOU*

Have you ever heard the term, "don't fight fire with fire?" My mom uses it all the time with Luna and me. When you add to a problem it can only grow larger. Soon you will  have a problem so out of control; you don't even know where to begin to end it. On the bus, if I were to have calmly and politely expressed my thoughts to the bus crowd or bus driver, rather than screaming, I would not have gone from being a victim to a bully. Instead, I was as much to blame as the Bus Crowd Bullies because I became angry and yelled mean words, which legally is called harassment.

When Wayne was hitting and kicking me, the rest of the Bus Crowd Bullies became accomplices to his bullying which was really a crime of assault and battery. An accomplice is someone who encourages the bully (Wayne) and the bullying behavior to continue. They also become liable and responsible for the crime. I also made it difficult to prove I was being bullied, since I then became a part of the bullying problem. In most cases, bullying is intentional aggressive behavior and it typically is repeated over and over again. Bullying can take many forms such as verbal, physical, and emotional bullying. On the bus I was intimidated, kicked, hit and verbally insulted; legally this would be called assault and battery, and harassment and it is illegal.

Don't miss → Also, the "not so innocent bystanders" were also bullying me because they watched everything happening and did nothing to stop it. Remember, you could be questioned as a witness if the victim is physically hurt and you watched the bullying.

In many states laws have been passed to protect and help a victim of bullying. Some state laws even consider harassment and intimidation as bullying. Also, even if you live in a state which has not passed specific anti-bullying laws, this does not mean you have to suffer in silence. Under federal and state laws of the United States Government you have protection from assault, battery, and harassment and you can press criminal charges.

Also, like I said in **Chapter 4**, under the laws of some states, a school district could be held liable and legally responsible if someone was hurt and the school knew the bullying was a problem. When it comes to the legal liability of a school district and the bus driver, this can be tricky because in most cases the bus driver is not an employee of the school, so the school is not liable when the students are riding the bus. (And let's face it, how can bus drivers really supervise the bus when they should be concentrating on their driving so all of the students are safe!)

Now to better understand some of these big criminal terms, let me try to make it easy: An *assault* is any attempt to threaten or injure

Legal → another person and is committed *without physical contact*. *Battery* requires physical contact of some sort (bodily injury or offensive touching) *without permission*. While *harassment* is defined as using words, gestures and actions which alarm or verbally abuse another person.

Also, to make something a crime you need two things—the intent and the act. Assault and battery and criminal harassment are all legal issues which can be prosecuted by law. Again, I ask you to please read my *Bullying Fact Sheet* in the back of this book; it really covers the whole topic of bullying and goes into detail about the legal side of bullying. Also, bullying was once considered a rite of passage, but now it's seen as a devastating form of abuse that can have long term effects on the victims self esteem. Bullying is a problem we want to decrease, not increase, so if you fight back by being a bully you have only escalated the problem and added another bully to the crowd.

What is the solution? Go to an adult and ask for help and remember there are laws in place to protect you so speak up—*don't suffer in silence!* most important

REMEMBER THIS!

School violence has been linked to bullying, and in our world today, it has become almost an epidemic. If your state has not taken this issue seriously and passed anti-bullying laws to protect children and youth, get busy and make some calls to your state representatives! We need to stop the bullying so we can stop the violence.

write to your congressman or congresswoman to implement bullying laws! The future is in Your Hands!

CHAPTER 6
I THOUGHT ONLY KIDS WERE BULLIES!

THE REAL DEAL

In a study done in urban elementary schools in the U.S.; 40% of the teachers admitted to bullying students and 3% said they bullied frequently. (HRSA)

40%—see Dorie's two cents

YOUR TWO CENTS

Question 1: Has a teacher, coach or school administrator ever bullied you or a friend?
Response: "At the time I didn't think so, but looking back it looks that way. I thought I was just being punished, but something about it just didn't feel right."
Question 2: Have you or a teammate ever been bullied on a sports team? If so, what happened and did the coach do anything?
Response: "Yes, I had friends tell me if I would lose a couple pounds I could run faster. That was when my little sister was a much better athlete and was doing much better than me. I became upset by the constant teasing from my teammates. The coach laughed at me and told me to quit being so sensitive."
Question 3: Has an adult ever made you feel bad about your body?
Response: "Yes!!!! My mom always comments on my nose. She says things like too bad you didn't take after my side of the family, like your brother did. Unfortunately, you have your dad's nose. Now whenever I look in the mirror all I can see is my big nose."

Dear Diary,

   Mom drove me to school today and I was really glad. It didn't seem to matter because at school, the Bus Crowd Bullies saw me and teased me because my mom drove me to school.

I can't win!! This time though, Alana and Cass helped defend me and we tried "group correction." Here's what happened.

I was alone by my locker getting ready for class. Luan, Suzy, Dana, Mark, Wayne and Joe were huddled together across the hall, taunting me because my mom drove me to school. Then, I saw from the corner of my eye, Alana and Cass racing to my rescue! They saw what was happening and reacted quickly! I stepped away from my locker and my friends jumped to my side, making a  circle. Then, we saw Nancy and Ash!! We motioned for them to join us and although they hesitated for a second, they came and stood next to Alana and Cass. I struck a pose, like Charlie's Angels, with my body standing tall and ready for action. Then, all five of us struck a defiant pose with hands on our hips. There I was in the middle, with the protective circle of my friends around  me!! We were ferocious looking girl superheroes defying the taunting Bus Crowd Bullies!

Luan, Suzy, Dana, Mark, Wayne and Joe were definitely impressed and backed away. For once, they stopped making fun of me and left me alone. Now I am CONVINCED there IS power in numbers.

Unfortunately, all of my friends live on the opposite side of town so there is no way we can all  ride my bus together. Also, my parents were informed by the school administration there was no way I could switch buses. This is a real shame because the group correction technique seems to be very useful in solving the bullying problem, and I feel more secure and comfortable with my friends by my side.

Dorie

-XOXO-

hope is here!

77

Dear Diary,

Today was the worst day!! I was thinking that being a secret agent, like in the movies, would be fun, but after this Charlie's Angels thing; forget it! All it did was get me in trouble!! When I was talking with Ms. Nechman, my counselor, about our "group correction technique" at school, Mr. Napoleon came in and asked to see me. Mr. Napoleon is our principal. His name isn't really Mr. Napoleon. I just call him this because he is very short mr . napolean like the French Emperor, Napoleon, and feels that he needs to assert power by making kids cry.

I had no idea why he wanted to talk with me, but I was pretty sure he was meeting with me to talk about my mother's phone call. I felt so relieved, he was here to help and finally the bus bullying would stop. He must have interviewed the "not so innocent bystanders" to collaborate my story and some brave student came to my rescue. I wasn't really nervous when he brought me to his office, so when he asked me to sit in the chair by his desk, I plopped down with a smile on my face and started fantasizing about what he might say. This may sound naive, but I had no negative experiences with Mr. Napoleon, so why should I expect the worst? My silly bubble of relief was burst when he uttered the following words, which started a nightmare.

"Dorie," he said, "Are you familiar with the students Wayne, Mark, Joe, Luan, and Suzy?"

"O, yes," I said and I thought to myself, yes, a "not so innocent bystander" came to my rescue. Maybe I would be given a chance to tell him what had been happening on the bus since last year and receive some help. I continued, "You know, I would really like to talk to you about them. Our bus rides together haven't been too good."

He grimaced and sat on top of his desk looking down at me. It was a little scary and very intimidating. "So I've heard." he said. "That is actually what I want

Zap

Zap

to talk to you about." So he did know what was going on! Yes, this would be my chance for help!!! In an odd voice he said, "I would like to ask you a few questions about it." When he said this, I got shivers up my spine; sort of a premonition of doom. His voice had changed and was harsh and demanding. He was also now standing over me and looking down. I looked at my hands and thought, something doesn't feel right.

"Let's begin, shall we?" he said.

I looked at him, nodded and added a little smile, but he just glared over his nose and down at me. The whole atmosphere of the room had changed, sort of like an electrical charge, and I was starting to feel its affects. My ears started ringing and I became a bit dizzy.

"Do you often talk to the people on your bus?" he asked.

"Well sometimes," I said, "Usually I'm telling them to leave me alone though." I added.

"Is it the other way around, ever?" he asked in an accusatory manner. What was happening; was he blaming me?

"No, not really." I said

"Yes or no." he barked. "Let me remind you that lying will get you no where and it is not accepted here." he said.

Again, I said no, but this time my lips began to quiver and I started stammering as I mumbled the words. I just looked at him and for some reason; I don't think this is about what I think it is.

"Why am I here, what's going on?" I said in a confused voice. If he was worried about me on the bus, he definitely would not be asking me these questions or talking in such a scary way.

"That is not important." he said. By now he was standing right in front of me and staring with a hard gaze that frightened me quite a bit.

"It's important to me and I don't understand why these questions are important to my problem on the bus." I said in a somewhat indignant tone.

"Hum," he said, "We'll see." So was he on my side or not? Maybe he is, but just wants to make sure I don't make up lies. That seems understandable, kind of.

"Did you ever tell them to leave you alone by saying 'shut your freaking trap'?" he asked.

"Well yes, but that's not how it happened."

"Oh really, that's not what I heard." he replied in a superior voice.

"I swear I'm telling the truth, you have to understand what really happened; go ask the others on the bus, I'm sure they will explain it. They attacked me first, I only yelled back because I felt like I was backed in a corner. They pushed me way too far this time and something inside just snapped. I know it was wrong, but I couldn't take it any more!" I said in one long exasperated voice.

"Dorie, why don't you just admit to the truth and quit wasting my time." he said in a bored manner.

"What truth? They tease me every single day and make the bus ride horrible. No one tells them to stop, everyone just sits and laughs and I'm tired of being the target. Why do you think my mom has tried to change my bus route? Really now, how could one girl bully such a large group, it doesn't make sense!"

"I will decide what makes sense." he replied in a confident manner, as if the conversation was over.

"Don't you care what happened to me? Can't I say anything to defend myself or is it their word against mine?" I blurted out in a state of panic.

"I see," he said and then added, "Yes or no will be sufficient."

80

Why doesn't he understand what "no" means, I have obviously already said it more than once!!

He followed this by a various amount of questions quoted from the speech I gave on the bus and other extremely ridiculous accusations. Such as, did I ever say their hearts were as black as coal; they were horrible people; Dana had to pay someone to go out with her; the bus crowd bullies had no life; and did I hit them? The stream of questions continued on and on, all the way through fourth period and when I finally thought he was done, he started from the top and repeated the same questions over and over again.

With each repetition, he became more forceful and I became more confused. His manner turned from questioning to accusatory and blaming in the blink of an eye and soon he was telling me what a horrible person I was and how I was lying to him. He kept saying I harassed others and there would be extra discipline consequences because I was denying it. Throughout the whole interrogation, he was standing above me and yelling into my face.

My legs turned to jelly, my body was shaking and my voice was squeaking in an uneven and high pitched quiver. My nose was starting to run and I was at the edge of tears. By the end of the whole two hour ordeal, I was admitting to things he accused me of and adding things I never even did. I was so exhausted that I hoped if I agreed with him, he would just let me go. Finally, he released me from this horrible torture and I left just as the bell was ringing. I walked out of his office unable to say anything or even think straight. I was in a trance and I was in shock. I just concentrated on gulping back the lump in my throat which was making me want to cry.

I AM NOT A LIAR

Diary, tonight I have gotten my balance somewhat back, but I still am feeling a little uneasy. My mom is very frustrated about how Mr. Napoleon handled the problem. She felt he did not look at both sides of the story and was disappointed no one else on the bus would stand up for me and tell the truth. How could she resolve the problem or even go to the police without evidence. It would be my word against everyone else's word and it would be difficult without the school's cooperation. I'm really nervous and my legs are a bit wobbly. Also, my stomach is churning and I feel somewhat nauseous. I don't think I want to go to school tomorrow (or ever again)!

Dorie

Dear Diary,

You know how I said yesterday was the worst day? I was wrong! Today was!! Now I know why Mr. Napoleon called me into his office. Diary, I'll start from the beginning. When I got on the bus this morning, I could tell something was wrong and I became nervous. Reason one; because nobody was making fun of me and reason two; the Bus Crowd Bullies were all smiling strangely. Edging on a smirk, but not a full out smirk. They all exchanged glances and evil smiles.

I went through the morning wondering what was going on and in the middle of the day, Mr. Napoleon asked to speak to me again. Something inside of me said this is not good, and now I was really nervous! I was becoming annoyed because he started asking the same questions as yesterday and we went through the whole routine one more time. I kept saying, "No and I'm confused, why you don't believe me?" I became very agitated and my voice started to break. I thought to myself, how many times do I need to say no!! Finally, he told me I was lying to him. All I could

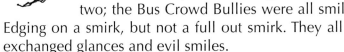

this is cruel + unusual punishment!

do was look at him in shock. Why in the world would I lie to him? How could he accuse me of lying when he never even looked at both sides of the story?

I continued to give him the same answer 50,000 times!!! Don't you think my story would break down if I was lying? Couldn't he tell my knees were shaking, why did he need to keep intimidating me?!? The entire time I kept telling myself, "What are you talking about, Mr. Napoleon, I am not lying," just so I could concentrate. He ignored my comments about being confused and started accusing me of "harassing my other bus members and being a bully."

No joke! Mr. Napoleon called ME a BULLY!! Who was the one doing the bullying in this conversation? The adult!!! Then he said I was an even worse person because I was lying about not being a bully and it would only make the problem worse. After he said this, I became extremely angry and indignant (which I still am).

1. I am not a bully! *Hello mr. Napoleon!*
2. I was bullied! *wake up!*
3. I do not lie and have never lied to a teacher. If he was so smart, he would know that I'm a terrible liar.
4. Doesn't my past behavior count for anything?
5. Why am I being punished for defending myself?

Nice Guy ——> Not!

The Bus Crowd Bullies, who had made my life miserable, had totally set me up because I decided to stand up for myself! They didn't like my friends supporting me by using the Charlie's Angels thing for "group correction," so this was their revenge! The worst part was Mr. Napoleon believed them and I now have (ONLY ME!!) multiple detentions. I sensed Mr. Napoleon wanted me to really break down and cry, but I wouldn't. I didn't allow his tirades to have this effect on me and throughout it all, I kept telling myself, "Just breathe and stay strong." I looked at him with defiant eyes and walked out of his office like I was the Queen of Sheba (ok, maybe not a bright idea), but how could he think ONE person could harass SIX people!!! Where were the witnesses, the "not so innocent bystanders?" This doesn't even make sense and why don't all six of us have detentions? Why just me?? Where's the justice?

When I arrived home, I told my mom, but she had already heard because the school had called about my detentions. She was really mad because every single day she saw my frustration with the bus and the school offered no support or suggestions to end this problem. I gave her my account of what happened with Mr. Napoleon and she was baffled why no one had come to my defense and why did the school not investigate the problem further.

Mom understood I had reached the breaking point and she was desperate to find a solution to the bus situation. She didn't exactly approve of my behavior, but understood I was tired of being the better person and ignoring the Bus Crowd Bullies. She believed everyone involved should be punished, not just me. She always says, "It takes two to tango!" So why don't the Bus Crowd Bullies ALSO have a detention, huh? cha cha cha

Again, where's the justice?

Mom called Mr. Napoleon again, but he wouldn't return her phone calls. Because of this, she is going to go to school tomorrow to talk with him in person. This is not fair and I'm really furious. I also feel really ashamed and I know I shouldn't be so hard on myself.

Angry does / even cut for It how I feel!

I know the Bus Crowd Bullies provoked me and I felt cornered, so I over reacted. What is the long-term result of my actions? What will other teachers think of me now? Before, I had a good reputation of being kind and caring!!!!!??! Diary, what will all the adults I respect now think of me?

Dorie

tear, tear, sniffle, tear, sniffle

DORIE'S TWO CENTS *FOR SURVIVING AN ADULT BULLY*

Don't Skip It is normal for us to be reprimanded by adults who love and care for us. This may include teachers, parents, relatives, neighbors, babysitters, and other caregivers. Sometimes it can make you feel a tad bit ashamed or sad, but usually after a good night sleep you are ready to change the behavior that caused the problem. This is normal behavior and we all make mistakes and learn from them.

Do you know a Mr. Napoleon? If you do, you may have met the childhood bully who has never matured emotionally and is now an adult bully. This bully can present himself or herself in many forms. It could be a sports coach screaming your performance is poor because you are too fat or the English teacher who tells you in a degrading manner you are too dumb to write a good essay. It could also be the person who insults you because of your family's lifestyle or religious choices.

Remember though, it is important you don't accuse a non-Mr. Napoleon of being a Mr. Napoleon because many times we may feel victimized only because we are being overly sensitive. You must look closely at the situation because often adults are really only trying to help us make the right decisions. Let's face it, we are still children and we are learning from our mistakes and adults are here to guide us along our journey to maturity. *Yes!* So before you over react, look closely and honestly at the situation or problem and if the adult in question matches with most of the points below, then you may have found an adult bully.

ADULT BULLY:

1. In front of other people, or alone, the person talks to you in a way that is very demeaning and embarrassing.

2. You feel physically threatened by the adult at times.

85

3. The level of anger and punishment far outweighs the actual situation. *Not good*

4. The person has a lack of physical or verbal control and may often scream or act in a way that is inappropriate for the situation. You may actually feel physically frightened or physically threatened.

5. The person doesn't respect your physical personal space or opinions.

REMEMBER THIS!   *Please Do!*

Just because you are in trouble, doesn't mean you are being bullied. If you do feel threatened, talk to a trusted adult you feel comfortable with and ask for help. Don't feel as if there is not an adult to talk with because if it's not a parent, it may be a teacher, family member, friend, or it could be the lunch lady at school or even the school bus driver. It could even be the woman, who lives next door, who gives you the creeps because of all her cats. Just ask, "Do you have a minute, because something is really bothering me and I don't *very true* know what to do." **You may not believe it, but it is in most people's nature to want to help,** even the people you least expect will surprise you with their love and concern!

CHAPTER 7
JUST BELIEVE ME!

THE REAL DEAL

Bullying can affect youth's self-esteem and feelings of worth. It also can increase their social isolation, leading them to become withdrawn and depressed. (NYVPRC)

Do you still want to bully?

YOUR TWO CENTS

Question 1: How do you deal with mean girls in your school?
Response 1: "I ignore them and stay away."
Response 2: "I try and make them like me so they will be nice to me."
Question 2: As a girl, are boys or girls bullying you most?
Response: "Mostly girls, but sometimes boys. The boys' will usually only bully with other girls."
Question 3: Do you ever become depressed from be bullied? What do you do?
Response 1: "It wasn't really a depression. I just kind of withdrew from things I normally would have done because I was afraid it would only lead to more bullying."
Response 2: "When I was bullied, I decided that if I remained happy the bullies would get annoyed and leave me alone. Unfortunately, after four months of bullying everyday that really wasn't an option."

Dear Diary,

Today, just as I expected, I'm getting a weird reaction at school. Some of my teachers gave me strange looks; it was a slight shake of the head and a tsk. They looked at me with disappointment, as if they were saying, "What a shame, I thought she was better than that."

tears roll on, days go by, D, now I wish I could fly.

I wanted to scream, "Of course I'm better than that!" I wanted to cry out, "Hey, why do you believe the Bus Crowd Bullies?" I kept asking myself, "Why won't the "not so innocent bystanders," the people who saw everything, the witnesses, stand up for me?" I've been there for them when THEY needed me? All of this was really terrible and upsetting. Why can't anyone realize the "not so innocent by standers" were actually reinforcing the story of the Bus Crowd Bullies by not telling the truth? The truth would rescue me and they had the power to do it!

Yesterday, when I asked Mr. Napoleon what actions of mine would be labeled harassing, he wouldn't answer. I ask you, Dear Diary, what type of principal won't explain the problem so it won't occur again? How can I learn from my mistakes? Now I'm going to get my first detention, EVER. I'm wondering how this is going to affect me going forward. When I apply for college, will admissions see this on my permanent record and reject me!!?!?! This is so unfair!!!!!!!! I am furious!!!! I wish the people on my bus would move away. I wish I could hide or disappear, at least move to another planet!! Every time I see the Bus Crowd Bullies at school, they make terrible faces at me. You can tell they are revelling in what happened and enjoying their power. All I did was defend myself (I admit a bit strongly) by standing up to THEIR BULLYING and they managed to turn the story completely around and convince the principal and the entire school that I'm a bully!! When I see the Bus Crowd Bullies at school, I just return their looks with fury in my eyes and try to hold back the tears. Thanks to them, now I'M going to get a reputation as a bully. I truly detest them!!!!!

But wait a minute...I need to calm down; this will not make it better. How do I calm down and make it better? Sometimes I wish I could get revenge, but then I would be lowering myself to their playing field and no matter what happens I will NEVER do *I wish I could disappear* that again. I must remember the best revenge in life is success. The whole school may think I'm a bully and a liar, but at least I know the truth. And my friends also know the truth. I can count on Alana, Cass, Nancy and Ash and that's all that matters.

Dorie ...or is it?

I HATE THE BUS

Dear Diary,

That's it, I'm done! I can't ride the bus anymore. It's a bully fest on the bus and I can't go back there. It's a no man's land of trouble. They tease and taunt me and if I say anything, they'll go tell Mr. Napoleon and I'm already in enough trouble with him. He won't think I've learned my lesson from the four deten- tions I served. Yes, 4!!!!!! Talk about unfair. When my mother went to visit Mr. Napoleon he wouldn't even listen to her account of what had been happening on the bus. He claimed he heard I was the bully and felt confident in the story he received. Mom felt very frustrated and angry that the school did not discipline everyone involved in the incident and when she explained this to him he replied, "There was no need to, Dorie was reported as the bully."

I served FOUR DETENTIONS for standing up for myself and now riding the bus is even worse because the bullies feel they have power and protection from the school. Wayne, one of the meanest bus bullies, hits and kicks me whenever he is close and everybody laughs. It's unbearable. Dana leads the insults and the whole Bus Crowd joins in with more laughs. The only relief I have is when I can find a seat up front by the bus driver which doesn't happen very often. They don't dare go after me in front of the bus driver because then they could be caught. Luna tries to stay close to me on the bus to offer protection, but it's sometimes impossible to find a seat for both of us. Also, I don't think any of the teachers believe my story and I am terrified and I feel so alone.

Why do people have a need to be mean?

It's my bus too, and I have every right to ride it without being scared. I told the bus driver how the Bus Crowd Bullies were treating me and he said,

"Maybe I should watch what I'm doing before I point a finger." I feel worse every day, and I'm beginning to think maybe I am a bad person, I don't even know anymore. I'm feeling sadder every day and I feel like I'm crying all the time. During meals, I just pick at my food and stare at my plate without bothering to talk. I am so tired I wish I could sleep for a thousand years. At night I just sit in my bedroom listening to music; I don't even bother to call my friends.

My mom can see the changes in me and how depressed I am and she is really worried. She keeps trying to talk about it, but I avoid her because I don't know how to explain how I feel. How do you explain EMPTY INSIDE!!? She and my dad don't have enough time to drive me to school, so she is upset the bus is so unsafe. I see concern on her face when I come home from school. Could I be causing this? Mr. Napoleon doesn't seem to care and refused to discuss the issue again with my mother. What am I going to do now? I don't know where to turn. I feel so alone. I wish I could just disappear!!!

Dorie

Dear Diary,

Is it possible to feel nothing?

I had a heart-to-heart talk with Ms. Nechman today; she is such a great counselor! Now I think she finally believes me!! She noticed I looked really depressed and said, "You should let it out and share the problem with me." So I told her everything, and by the end I was bawling uncontrollably. I couldn't help it. She sat there somewhat dumbfounded and it took her a few minutes to piece everything together. My problem must have had a big impact on her by the way she reacted. Below I wrote what I said so you, Diary, can make your own judgment.

Thank goodness for Ms. Nechman.

My conversation with Ms. Nechman:

It was the middle of the day and I was on my way to Algebra when Ms. Nechman stuck her head out of her office and called me in. Naturally, I thought I was in more trouble, but it was not to be the case. She told me she just wanted to talk, and when I asked why she said it was because I looked like I needed too. She was right, but I wasn't sure if I could tell her what had happened. Would she even believe me or would it be a waste of time?

I took a deep breath and observed her guidance room I knew so well. The door opens to the right of the room, and directly to the right of the door is a window looking out towards the hallway (it has blinds that are usually drawn). When you walk past the door on the right wall is a book shelf, and on the left wall is a painting. The far back wall has two windows looking over the parking lot and a filing cabinet on the left. Ms. Nechman's desk is in front of the windows and the students have the outside view, while she views artwork from students that is taped all over her filing cabinets.

Finally, I couldn't restrain myself much longer so I started talking. Ms. Nechman just sat there listening and didn't say a word until I was finished. I thought it would be hard, but the words flew out of my mouth one after another, I couldn't stop! Soon, tears were flowing down my cheeks and I had to take breaks to wipe my nose with a tissue. I started with the first day of school and led up to Mr. Napoleon yelling at me because he thought I was lying. I told her everything, from my tripping on the first day and being teased to the bus bullying lately. I even told her how my mom had called the school repeatedly and there was no cooperation from Mr. Napoleon. I explained that even my parents were at a loss to solve the bullying and were ready to contact the police for help.

Wow, did this get her attention and she said she would step in and help solve the problem on the bus. I couldn't stop myself, it was if a flood gate broke inside and there was no holding back. When I had finished she just sat there for a few minutes soaking it in and maybe waiting to see if I had anything else to say.

When she spoke, the words she said gave me great relief and after many days of misery, I finally found some peace of mind. "Your story makes sense now. I didn't think you where the type of girl to harass your whole bus because you've never behaved like that in the classroom."

I half smiled through my tears and thanked her for believing me. What a relief to tell somebody the story who really knew me. Maybe NOW things can change. Finally, someone believes me besides my family. She said she was going to talk to Mr. Napoleon as soon as possible. Diary, I think there actually may be hope for me on the bus and in school.

Dorie   XOXOXOXO

DORIE'S TWO CENTS *FOR SURVIVING DEPRESSION*

Life is long and there is a lot of time to make mistakes and fix them. If you have no ailments, the average body is meant to live to the age of one hundred and twenty-years old and if you live to this age, you're going to have many problems along the way. You need to learn how to solve your problems in a positive and healthy way and there is always a solution to your problems, even when you think there isn't. When you are feeling depressed, you often can't think clearly so you can't accurately see solutions to your problems. If you ever feel like you don't want to live anymore, talk to a trusted adult who can offer help. You have a long life ahead of you and why give up when you're so young. Also, giving in to depression is like saying "you win" to those who are tormenting you. Why give bullies this satisfaction? I personally would not want to allow Wayne, Mark, Dana and the rest of the

Bus Crowd Bullies to have the satisfaction of cheating me out of my life. Remember, middle school and high school years are only seven years of your life. You can sur-vive, but please ask for help if you are feeling depressed!

IF you're skimming, don't forget this !!!

REMEMBER THIS!

Sometimes you may not realize that you are depressed until it is too late. If you are feeling depressed, seek out help from a trust-ed adult. They want to help you and have the skills to help. Life is worth living!

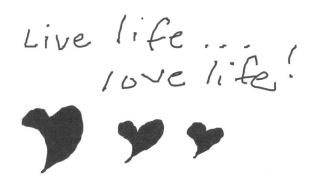

Live life ... love life!

CHAPTER 8
THE DIFFERENCE
ONE PERSON CAN MAKE!

THE REAL DEAL

Just as society doesn't expect victims of other types of abuse to "deal with it on their own," we should not expect this of victims of bullying. Adults play a critical role in stopping bullying. (HRSA)

YOUR TWO CENTS

So please help!

Question 1: If you were bullied, did it affect your grades?
Response 1: "Yes it did."
Response 2: "Not really, it made me concentrate more on my school work because I didn't really have any friends to distract me. Not that I would trade better grades for friends."
Question 2: Have you had one person make a difference in your life when you were being bullied? Who was it and what did they do?
Response 1: "Yes, a friend told some girls to stop gossiping about me."
Response 2: "My sister always talks to me about the problem and makes me feel better."

Dear Diary,

Yesterday, Ms. Nechman said she took care of the whole bullying problem for me. The Bus Crowd Bullies all had detentions and were told if they harassed me on the bus again, they could face *I* suspension. She also called my mom and apologized *am* for the way the problem was handled and assured her the harassment on the bus would stop. I wonder *So* if they finally took action because I said my parents were thinking about contacting the police. Did the *happy!!* school become worried there would be some big investigation or possibly a lawsuit? I may never know, but I'm sure glad she put a stop to the power of the Bus Crowd Bullies. I felt like giving her a hug and I thanked her a million times. I was so grateful I even wrote her a thank you letter and dropped it by her office later in the day.

I don't think I've felt this happy in a long time. Today, for the first time, the Bus Crowd Bullies left me alone. All they did was glare at me!! It was so great, I don't think I've actually enjoyed (somewhat) a bus ride more. Ms. Nechman is the best and I don't know what I would do without her!

Dorie

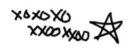

Dear Diary,

Things have been going really well!! I'm starting to feel like myself again and my grades are improving! I feel so much safer in school and on the bus. Cass, Alana, Nancy, Ash and I are going to have a sleepover to celebrate. We're going to watch my favorite movie and eat my favorite foods! I'm so happy I could start singing, so I think I will. Now I have to stop though, because Luna just rapped on my door about twenty times and told me to shut up because she's trying to sleep.

Maybe I shouldn't go into the singing career! Diary, nighty night.

Dorie

Dear Diary,

We had loads of fun at the sleepover, but I'm too tired to write.

Dorie

Dear Diary,

Another good day, the Bus Crowd Bullies were sending me evil glares, but I didn't care one bit. All I care is that I'm safe and there is no way they can touch me now. They thought they were so smart, well I outsmarted them by talking to Ms. Nechman. Therefore, I get the last laugh. HA!! Not that I wanted to get them in trouble, but the bullying needed to stop. Diary, I really believe good behavior and the truth triumphs!

Dorie   yippyde deodle day!

DORIES' TWO CENTS *FOR SURVIVING AND UNDERSTANDING YOUR SIGNIFICANCE IN ANOTHER'S PERSON'S LIFE*

One person can really make a difference in another person's life. Just a smile or a kind word can brighten up somebody's day. Sometimes we don't realize how deeply our actions can affect another person, but a small and polite gesture can make all the difference. Here's a story I once heard from a very wise person.

There once was a man down on his fortune and nothing seemed to be going well in his life. He decided the only way to end his bad fortune was to end his life and he sat down on a park bench deep in thought. The same day a stranger who was up on his luck decided to take a stroll through the park. On his walk, he noticed the man down on his luck sitting on the bench. The stranger walked up to him and said, "Good morning" in such a happy voice the man sitting on the bench looked up in wonder and confusion. He thought to himself, "Why had this stranger even cared to talk to me and why was he so happy?" The man returned the greeting and went back into deep thought. The stranger could have walked off, but instead he realized the other man was in need of help because he looked so desolate. He said, "Sir, tell me what troubles you." Again, the man looked at him in awe. Why did this complete stranger even care about him? He answered, "I'm not up on my luck." The stranger looked at him and said something that would forever change the man's life. He said, "My good fellow, do not look at it as if you are out of luck. You have only hit a rough patch, but things will turn around in time. When life gives you lemons; make lemonade." The stranger turned and walked away, leaving the man sitting on the bench very confused but hopeful and glad to be alive. Yes, he had hit a rough patch, but things can always become better. Something sour can become sweet.

What can we learn from this story? We can learn a few things such as: 1. From the stranger we are taught just small greetings and inquiries on the state of another person can make a big *hello* difference. It can even change the direction and outlook of someone's life. 2. From the man down on his luck, we learn everything negative can become positive. *Yes!* When life gives you something sour, instead of just accepting it and giving up, add some sugar and make it sweet. Close your eyes; open them and look at the situation from a new perspective. You just might find something sweeter. This happened to me when I realized there is no reason to stay depressed and give up hope because all I had to do was find the right people to help me straighten out the problem. Ms. Nechman helped me and I was able to make a negative situation into a positive situation. Also, through everything I had the support and love of my family, even when I felt alone. (Even Luna cared enough to help!!)

REMEMBER THIS! *So Sweet*

Lemons make lemonade; you only have to add a touch of your own sugar. Also, everyday try to make a positive difference in someone else's life. Take the time to be kind and notice when someone needs your help. Not only will they feel better, but you will feel better. It would take so little effort to smile and say something kind. The world would become a better place if we all cared for the feelings of others. *♥ + ♡ = (xxoo)*

CHAPTER 9
HIGH TECH BULLYING:
COMPUTER + BULLY = COWARD!

THE REAL DEAL

this # is way 2 big!

In an online survey of about 1,500 internet using youths, 12.6% reported they had been threatened physically online and almost 5% reported they were scared for their safety. (www.cyberbullying.us)

YOUR TWO CENTS

Question 1: Have you or a friend ever been cyber bullied? What did you do? How did it make you feel? Did you tell anybody?

Response 1: "I was, but I didn't tell anybody or do anything because I thought it happened to everyone. Now I know it was wrong and I should have told someone."

Response 2: "I was cyber bullied by my best friends. I didn't realize it was them until I told my mom. She helped me find out who it was. I'm glad I told someone."

Question 2: Would you ever tattle on a bully? Why or why not?

Response 1: "Yes, if it came to a point the bullying was dangerous."

Response 2: "I don't think I would. Sometimes it just makes the problem worse."

Question 3: Have you ever cyber bullied somebody? Why?

Response: "No I haven't. I don't think it's very nice but some of my friends have. It was very hard being stuck in the middle. I wanted to do the right thing, but I didn't want to lose a friendship. In the end I did lose their friendship, but I gained the friendship of their victim."

Dear Diary,

I've started to get some really weird Instant Messages on the computer and it's totally creepy. I don't know who they're from, but they say stuff like, "Beware!" and, "You'll regret what you did." I don't answer the messages and have decided to block them, but I keep receiving new ones from different screen names. It's scaring me so I told my mom and she said I should stop ASAP Instant Messaging. Even though it pains me to say this, she's right. I shall quit and hopefully the threats will stop.

Dorie   *CREEPY?*

Dear Diary,

Whoever was sending me the Instant Messages is now sending them to my e-mail and they are becoming even scarier. They say, "If I tell someone I will be seriously injured." How dumb do I look? I think I could be injured if I don't tell someone. I told my mom and she told me to (again) ASAP quit using my e-mail and she would look into the problem because she was very concerned.

I have a feeling it's the Bus Crowd Bullies with a new form of revenge, so I decided to talk with Ms. Nechman. She agrees that it could be the Bus Crowd Bullies, but we shouldn't point fingers or make accusations unless we know for sure. She's right, but I'm not quite sure what to do, it's really scary. It makes me feel like someone is watching me but I don't know who. I don't like feeling I need to watch my every move. What if it's not the Bus Crowd Bullies? What if it's someone I don't even know? How am I going to find the underlying cause of these threats?

Dorie   *OK I'm scared!*

Dear Diary,

I received even scarier messages today, such as, "We know you told people and you had better stop. We're not joking or else you're going to get hurt." The weird part was after I read this, there was a rap on my window and a note was left saying, "We're watching you." Talk about extremely creepy. I pulled down my window shades and I was so scared I went to find Mom.

We have decided we need to talk to the police tomorrow. This may sound stupid, but I think it's the only way to ensure my safety. Mom and Dad agree, and they are both going to come with me to the station. I don't think I have ever been this afraid! I shouldn't be such a scaredy cat, but I am. I don't even want to sleep in my own room, so Luna said I could sleep in her trundle bed. I never thought she cared so much about me. Who knew? Diary, I better go tuck in before she changes her mind.

Dorie   xoxoxoxoxo

Dear Diary,

It has become super scary and my parents want to know who the cyber bully is... I mean, what type of person sends you messages telling you to "Kill yourself and you're life is not worth living." My parents are tracing the screen name and e-mail address with the police. I have a new screen name and e-mail address, but my parents asked me not to use it for now and to not tell anybody about my new e-mail address. It sounds so stupid to get my parents involved, but it comes to a point when they are the only ones who can help. I must admit, it is also quite embarrassing having the police involved, but when things get too big to handle, you really need somebody who has more experience.

Dorie

Dear Diary,

It turns out the people cyber bullying me were the Bus Crowd Bullies; Luan, Suzy, Dana, Mark and Wayne. My parents decided not to make a big deal out of this, but instead talked to their parents with the police present. The police explained cyber bulling is serious business with serious

consequences. Can you imagine the police coming to your house? I hope the problem with the Bus Crowd Bullies will finally end. I must say, this school year has not been the best! Diary, bedtime, thanks for listening.

Dorie

DORIE'S TWO CENTS *FOR SURVIVING CYBER BULLYING*

Cyber bullying has become a very big problem in our society. If you watch or read the news, the number of stories is overwhelming concerning teen suicides due to cyber bullying. A lot of teens do not know how to deal with this growing problem. Many people, adults included, say just ignore it or tell the person to stop, but anybody who has been a victim of cyber bullying knows *Be Safe* this approach seldom works. If people are making remarks or threats, either in person or on the computer, and this is hurting your feelings, scaring you or affecting your self-confidence, please tell a trusted adult.

Many times when you ask a bully to stop, the problem only escalates and adult intervention is needed. Cyber bullying is serious and needs to be addressed because it is a problem that won't "just go away on its own." You cannot ignore bullying and say, "it doesn't matter," because deep inside your heart you know it does and it can affect your self-confidence. If you ever feel threatened or have been threatened, immediately tell an adult. Also, don't ever feel embarrassed to involve law enforcement, they are here to help and they often have many resources you may not be aware of to assist with bullying. Bullying, harassment and violence is on the rise in our schools and many government agencies and resources are designed to put an end or assist with this crisis. If you are receiving anonymous threats, law enforcement may be able to find the source of the threats or at least offer suggestions to keep you safe.

REMEMBER THIS!

Don't ever think there is nothing that can be done to stop bullying.
Tell an adult and be positive change can happen because there is
always hope. Also, never even contemplate suicide or revenge as a
way to end the pain of bullying. My life matters, your life matters,
all of our lives matter! As they say, "where there is a will, there is a
way," it just may take some time and trust in those who love and care
for us. Remember what I said, middle school and high school are
only seven years of our life. Hang in there!

You can do it !!,
xxoo Dorie

CHAPTER 10
CASS, INTERNET SAVVY?
I DON'T THINK SO!

THE REAL DEAL

Peer pressure is not a bad thing. We are all influenced by our peers, both negatively and positively. The difference between negative and positive peer pressure is the outcome. (About.com)

YOUR TWO CENTS

Question 1: Have you ever used peer pressure to bring about positive changes in someone's behavior?
Response: "Yes, my friends and I talked to a friend who was doing dumb things to try to get her to stop." *good idea*
Question 2: Do you consider peer pressure good or bad?
Response: "I think it can be good and bad considering how it is used."

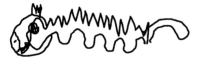

Dear Diary,

After the bus and cyber bullying fiasco, I have settled back into the swing of school and everything seems to be going well. My friends and I are getting along, but I'm starting to get worried about Cass. I've been so preoccupied with my own problems; I have failed to see what is going on with her. She is spending so much time on the computer, it's like she's addicted. I know she enjoys Instant Messaging and Nanopets but she can also do other things, but she doesn't want to, not even calling me. *one* What girl my age doesn't love the phone! Something *thing* isn't right and I am going to find out. *to the next*

Dorie

Dear Diary,

Today I talked to Alana about Cass. She agrees Cass's actions are worrisome, so we put our heads together and decided to think about how we should handle this problem. We realized in the past, Cass mentioned how you can meet people on Nanopets and talk with them on Instant Messaging. Maybe that's what she is doing?

Alana came up with a plan (Plan Alana) in which I will causally start talking about the people you can meet on Nanopets and try to prod some information out of Cass. If things aren't working as planned, I will do the special symbol (tug my hair, itch my nose and then sneeze). When Alana sees the special symbol, she will sit down and start talking about how she made a Nanopet Account and all the cool people she has met, especially a boy. By the way Diary, this never happened to Alana, it's just the bait.

Dorie

hope it works!

Dear Diary,

Today I was going to do Plan Alana (that's the plan Alana came up with yesterday), but something else came up to defer it. Carry and Sally, the most popular of The Popular girls in school, came up to me and wanted to talk. It appears that Cass was talking to them about her internet relationships which Alana and I suspected. I knew Cass was friends with them, but I didn't know they were such good friends. Anyway, it turns out she was doing more than we thought. She actually sent pictures to her internet "buddies," who are people she doesn't even know, and now wants to meet them in person!!!!! DANGER!! STUPID!! Does she want to die?? I wouldn't!! I couldn't believe it!

The four of us agreed this needed to stop, so I told Carry and Sally about Plan Alana, and we changed the plan a bit to

DANGER

adapt to a bigger group of people. Alana and I will follow the original Plan Alana and try to convince Cass to stop her dangerous activities. Since Cass told Sally and Carry earlier about her internet relations, they are going to skip the original Plan Alana and try to convince Cass to stop, explaining how she could be in danger. We decided revised Plan Alana (now called Plan A) would be put into effect tomorrow and we will rendezvous during study hall. I filled Alana in on the plan and she felt happy The Popular people agreed with her idea (somewhat, since they are really two different plans). I hope our revised Plan A goes well, but only time can tell. Diary, better get my sleep, big day tomorrow!

Dorie

Dear Diary,

Plan A seemed to go well, but I'm not so sure. Carry, Sally, Alana and I all had similar results. Cass seemed to be annoyed because we would not quit badgering her to stop her dangerous internet conversations, but she said she would stop. Alana and I didn't really believe her, even though Carry and Sally seemed convinced. It was something in the way she agreed to stop. It was the kind of agreement you use with your mother when she is nagging you to do something, and you just say you'll do it so she'll leave you alone.

We convinced Carry and Sally we needed to do some more research to make sure Cass wasn't lying, which Alana and I were pretty sure she was doing. So on Friday, the four of us are getting together to make a fake Nanopets Account and flirt with Cass to see what she does. If she gives away too much information, wants to send pictures or meet, then we know Alana and I are right. Diary, I know it's wrong to make a fake account and pretend to be someone else, but we are so worried about Cass. We just want her to be safe and we can't protect her if we don't know what she is up to. Please forgive me and I promise it won't happen again. Wish us luck and I'll keep you posted.

Dorie

DORIE'S TWO CENTS *FOR SURVIVING MISTAKES AND PEER PRESSURE*

yes
we
do !

Everybody makes mistakes. It's normal and you shouldn't beat yourself up about your errors. If you make a mistake, learn from it and move on. Sometimes, we notice people close to our hearts have made a mistake that could result in real future problems if it is not stopped. You may have a friend like Cass, who made a mistake, and was not able to see what she or he did was wrong. When a friend makes an error, it is sometime good to use peer pressure for positive results in behavior.

When you hear "peer pressure" you (if you have health classes in school like mine) probably automatically think, "peer pressure; bad." This can be true at times, but not with all occasions. It is bad to pressure someone into doing something dangerous or extremely against their will, but when you are trying to nudge them in the right direction, for their health and safety; it can be acceptable and successful. When you use peer pressure positively, you are encouraging someone to make the right decision. Carry, Sally, Alana and I used peer pressure to convince Cass to stop talking to complete strangers on the internet. In the end, positive or negative peer pressure won't always change the problem the person is facing because they may not want to listen and change their behavior. Don't feel guilty because every person has the final decision concerning their behavior and how they choose to live their life. Though positive peer pressure can greatly influence a situation, the person's mind makes the final decision. We each shape our own lives by the decisions we make everyday!

read this ~ make healthy choices

REMEMBER THIS!

Don't feel afraid to involve adults because they have a lot more tricks up their sleeve to solve problems than you do. This is called life experience! Also remember, we all make mistakes as we are growing up so try to practice patience and tolerance. At the same time, be concerned if a friend is making choices that are dangerous and destructive to themself and others. Get help because intervention often works best in the early stages of the problem. People have a hard time making changes when a problem becomes a habit!

good habits please!

CHAPTER 11
I WAS ONLY TRYING TO HELP!

THE REAL DEAL

When teens receive messages online from someone they don't know, 40% reported that they'll usually reply and chat with that person. Only 18% said they'll tell an adult. (NCMEC)

not smart!

YOUR TWO CENTS

Question 1: Has peer pressure ever changed a decision you made?
Response 1: "Yes. It was a big mistake to listen to my peers."
Response 2: "Yes, I was glad I listened."
Question 2: Has a stranger approached you online? What did you do?
Response 1: "Yes, I talked for awhile, but quit when he wanted my photo."
Response 2: "Someone weird started talking online to me and I became scared, so I blocked him."

Dear Diary,

I was right! I knew it! Of course I was, I know my friends and I can tell when they lie to me!! Diary, here is the conversation we had on Nanopets with Cass. Alana, Carry, Sally and I are skaterdud459 and Cass is cassforev2530.

I am right! hahaha

Cassforev2530: hey
Skaterdud459: hey
Cassforev2530: I'm Cass. Wats ur name?
Skaterdud459: I'm Luke
Cassforev2530: cool. Where are you from?
Skaterdud459: westbrook, u?

Cassforev2530: omg, me 2!!! Do u go to private?
Skaterdud459: ya u?
Cassforev2530: No, I go to public
Skaterdud459: O, that's cool
Cassforev2530: ya
Skaterdud459: do u play any sports
Cassforev2530: ya I play lax
Skaterdud459: o kool. U must be on varsity
Cassforev2530: no jv. I wish
Skaterdud459: don't worry u'll get there.
Cassforev2530: thx
Skaterdud459: If u want, I could help u get better
Cassforev2530: do u play lax?
Skaterdud459: ya my dad is coach of varsity. We're 12-0
Cassforev2530: wow
Skaterdud459: ya
Cassforev2530: that's so cool
Skaterdud459: so I could help u
Cassforev2530: that would be so cool
Skaterdud459: y don't we work smthng out
Cassforev2530: sounds great
Skaterdud459: give me ur sn and we can talk more
Cassforev2530: k its laxgirl45
Skaterdud459: cool
Cassforev2530: wats urs
Skaterdud459: skatelife245
Cassforev2530: great ttyl
Skaterdud459: yup

CASS ≠ INTERNET Savvy

With this conversation, I realized Cass was dumb and quite vulnerable. None of us knew what to do so we said we'd think things over during the weekend and get back to each other on Monday. Personally, I had no idea what to do and was pretty sure they felt the same way, so I thought it best to ask my mom for advice. Mom said this problem was escalating and could only become worse and possibly dangerous. She said it was beyond intervention from friends and we needed to make Cass's parents aware. The problem

blah!
blah!
blah!

was none of our parents knew Cass's mom very well, and we didn't know how she would react to the news (rumor has it, she has a hot temper) so we needed some other way of contacting her parents. My mom thinks the best idea is to talk to Ms. Nechman, my counselor, and she can talk the problem over with Cass and her parents. If Alana, Carry, Sally and I don't involve adults we trust, Cass may continue her foolish internet relationships and be in danger. I hate to admit it, but my mom is right. I thought I would never have to say it, but look at me; I'm saying it! I have no idea what is going to happen so wish me loads of luck. Diary, thanks for dealing with me.

Dorie

XOXOXO

Dear Diary,

Today Carry, Sally, Alana and I talked with Ms. Nechman and she said we did the right thing. Alana and I are trying to anticipate how Cass will react; we have absolutely no idea. Nancy and Ash have no idea what's going on so when Cass didn't sit with us at lunch, but glared from the other side of the lunchroom, they couldn't understand why.

Alana and I knew what Cass was up to because she was sitting with the Drama Club. If you want gossip spread, they are the people to go to. Soon they were making astonished faces and looking over at us quite frequently. I tried to ignore them, but it was really difficult. We finally had to tell Ash and Nancy what had happened, so they wouldn't feel so out of it. I saw Cass talking with Ash and Nancy later on and I don't know if they believed us, but I hope they did. All I can say is at least I have Alana as a true friend.

Dorie

DORIE'S TWO C_ _ _ _ _ _ _ _ _ _ _ _ _

THE NOT SO SAFE INTERNET

The internet isn't always as safe as it appears. You may think you're talking with a teenage boy your age, but you could really be talking with a fifty year old man. When I say this to my friends, they laugh at me and say, "Dorie, come on. Do you always have to think of the worst case scenario?" They can say this all they want, but they know I have a point. How do you know who you're talking with? You're not looking at their face, your looking at a computer screen. The picture they send you may not be theirs. Many young girls have been abducted by their so-called "internet boyfriends" who they have never even met. It happens all the time. Below I made a fake profile and let's pretend it's yours. Watch me figure out where you live—and possibly more!

WESTFIELD CLOVERS ALL THE WAY!!!! #22
LAX ROXS!!!!!
B THERE OR B SQUARE!!!
CHAMPIONSHIP 09!!!!

This may not seem like a lot of information, but it is! Now watch me find other details about you from this profile. I know you live in Westfield and play lacrosse; your number is 22. I first find the website for Westfield Lacrosse. I check which teams are going or went to the championships. If there isn't a website for lacrosse, the lacrosse championship information will most likely be in the town or regional newspaper. I go to the newspaper website or find an old newspaper. Usually, the names of the players are listed with their numbers in the newspaper photos. From there, I go to the yellow pages and look up your last name and I am probably able to find your phone number and address. From this information, I am able to find out where you live. Even with only a name, I can probably find your address. If I do Google Maps, I can see what your house looks like and maybe even your car. Freaked

this is creepy!

111

out yet?? If I'm only a teenage girl imagine what a predator, who does this all the time, could do? It's something you should think about because there are a lot of sexual predators who are on the internet and looking for their next victim. Be smart and stay safe; don't have conversations on the internet with people you don't know.

Think → don't stink!

REMEMBER THIS!

Next time you go to the internet service you use to keep in touch with friends, think about what you post online and say to strangers. Whatever you put on the internet is there FOREVER, for the whole world to see!! Do you really want to make yourself *Very* this vulnerable? Once you are in cyber space you are *Scary* forever in cyber space!

CHAPTER 12
YOU CALL IT RUMORS.
I CALL IT FUMORS
(THAT'S FALSE RUMORS).

THE REAL DEAL

The most common form of bullying is verbal bullying (teasing or name calling). Girls are more likely to report being targets of rumor-spreading and sexual comments. (HRSA)

YOUR TWO CENTS

Question 1: How do you deal if your so-called best friend starts spreading rumors about you and denies it?
Response 1: "Find a new best friend."
Response 2: "Just ignore it, it will pass, hopefully."
Question 2: Have you ever spread false rumors about a close friend? If so, are you still friends?
Response 1: Yes, because I was jealous. We did make up, but it has never been the same." *bad move!*
Response 2: "I did and I regret it because I lost a really close friend."

Dear Diary,

Today was not a very good day. Stella and the rest of the Drama Club spread rumors about whatever Cass had said, and everybody was talking about Alana and me (in a not so nice way). Now, I don't mind people talking about me, but I do mind when they are talking badly about me. The worst thing is we have no idea what they are talking *why believe it?!* about. Ash and Nancy are being very flimsy and are not standing by our side because they don't want to get involved. No one said they needed to get involved, but when someone is trash talking their best friends, they could at least tell them to knock it off! It's hard because whenever I walk into a hallway or classroom, people look at me and start whispering and making faces. I don't like it one bit and it needs to stop! It makes me feel so insecure; I hate when I feel awkward! Cass just walks around with a smirk on her face. I thought we were friends? Why did she do this to Alana and me?

My mom called her mom quite a few times to talk about the situation and express her concern for Cass, but she wouldn't return the calls. My mom said to me, "all children face challenges at times and adults are here to help." She really didn't know Cass's Mom well, but she wanted to extend a helpful hand. Finally, Cass's Mom did call, but she kind of freaked out on my mom (Diary, I guess the temper rumor was true). You would think she would thank us for being concerned, but instead she was angry and felt we embarrassed her family. She also went on about how I was such a bad friend to tell on Cass, and how poor Cass comes home every-day crying.

Um, hello! I think it's the other way around!! Clearly, Cass's Mom is getting an abridged story. The funny part was later on Cass's Dad called and thanked us. I don't think he knew about his wife's phone call to Mom. He called the police to track Cass's computer "buddies," and it turns out her friend "Mr. Nanopet" was a registered pedophile with a criminal record!

OUCH

XOXO
why do I feel both?

Even though it has put me in the middle of negative gossip, I am glad we did the right thing. Who knows what could have happened to Cass if we didn't do anything. Sometimes the right thing comes at a price, and you don't always have people knocking on your door thanking you. Often, all you get as a thank you is a warm feeling inside that makes you happy you did the right thing. It scares me to think what could have happened to Cass. Diary, if she would have met "Mr. Nanopet," she could be dead right now. Very scary!!!

Dorie

DORIE'S TWO CENTS *FOR SURVIVING GOSSIP*

bottom line

Gossiping is really cruel! It is possibly one of the worst forms of bullying and studies have shown it is one of the biggest contributors to school violence. What makes gossiping so annoying is people often believe what they hear, even if it is ridiculous. If somebody started a rumor saying you were moving to Antarctica to raise cattle somebody would probably believe it, even if it doesn't make sense because cattle are not raised in Antarctica because it is almost entirely covered by ice. We need to remember even though gossip can be hurtful and destructive, it is short lived. There is always a new stream of gossip to replace the old. Personally, I don't believe gossip and if I hear something really funky, I go and ask the person to clarify so I don't believe the wrong thing. When you are the center of gossip, it can be very hurtful. Also, it can be hard to find where the rumor started. For a quick fix, follow a few of these tips for surviving negative gossip about you.

SURVIVING NEGATIVE GOSSIP:

very important

1. When you know people are talking about you, hold your head high and walk with pride. Fake it until you make it. People don't have to know what you're feeling on the inside. Walk past people looking like you could care less because you feel good about yourself. Eventually, you won't have to fake it.

2. If someone confronts you about gossip concerning you, don't over react and become upset. Act really calm like it's no big deal, and if you act like it isn't a big deal, so will the others. You could

say something like, "Does that sound like me? Come on, what's your source? A gossip magazine?" Adding a joke will make them laugh and possibly eliminate tension. Also, they will walk away thinking kindly of you because they are thinking of your joke.

3. If you hear good friends gossiping about you, don't be afraid to kindly and calmly confront them. Don't go into the conversation with an accusatory attitude, because then your friends will automatically deny involvement in the rumors. Tell them how it made you feel when you heard them gossiping about you, such as, "I feel hurt because I heard you gossiping about me." Starting the conversation with "I feel" instead of "You did," and "My feelings were hurt," will make the person more open to apologize.

4. If your friends continually gossips about you, it may be time to reconsider your friendships and find new friends.

REMEMBER THIS!

Gossiping is more effective for the person gossiping if the victim becomes upset. It's what the person gossiping wants! By ignoring gossip, you help the gossip stop faster. If it doesn't stop and continues over a long period of time, don't be afraid to get help from a trusted adult because they are always there to help.

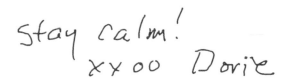

Stay calm!
xx oo Dorie

CHAPTER 13
HAVEN'T YOU EVER HEARD, "DON'T BELIEVE EVERYTHING YOU HEAR?" APPARENTLY NOT!

THE REAL DEAL

Girls often bully other girls by spreading gossip and encouraging others to exclude another girl. (NYVPRC)

YOUR TWO CENTS

Question: Why do you gossip about other girls?
Response 1: "I don't know we just do." *read this*
Response 2: "When I have gossip people pay attention to me. Without it, no one will even give me the time of day. I know it's bad, but now I just can't stop."
Response 3: "When someone looks threatening (they may take away my popularity) I spread rumors so no one will talk to them. Like the time when I was running for class president, there was another girl running who people really liked, so I spread some rumors about her and no one voted for her."

Dear Diary,

Alana and I just realized something; Cass doesn't know Carry and Sally also told on her, so Alana said we should go ask them to stop the gossip. She was right, because if anyone could help quell rumors, it would be The Populars. Unfortunately, Carry and Sally decided "they had no idea what we were talking about." Since they were of no help, I need-ed to at least find out what people were saying about Alana and me so we could end the gossip. Kind of stupid of me not to think of this before! I went to the Drama Club during lunch and asked if I could sit with them. I was pretty sure they were going to say no, so I sat down before they answered and said thanks. I could tell they weren't happy to have me at their table, but too bad, I had a job to do. I looked back at my table where I usually sit and Cass had taken my place; I suspected to talk about me. She makes me feel confused because we have been best friends forever, why is she acting this way? All I tried to do was help her be safe; I don't want my best friend dead! Is this how you re-pay your best friend for possibly saving your life?

I saw Alana frowning and she didn't look happy. Good old Alana, she always sticks up for me, and I don't know what I would do without her.

Ok, back to what I was doing with the Drama Club. I felt like an undercover agent looking for in-formation in another country. Just one slip up of a word and it would be all over. I had to watch my ev-ery move; very critical. I had to leave the table with the information I needed. As they all exchanged annoyed glances, I started asking about them to get a conversation going. I was on a mission which needed to be completed.

Stella started talking about her new role in the school play, but she suddenly stopped and asked the question I knew she eventually would, "Dorie, what happened with you and Cass?"

Bingo, this was what I came for. Now was the time to stop the rumors.

I looked at her and asked, "Stella, what have you been told?" because I was not going to give away too much, too soon. I didn't want to start MORE unnecessary rumors!

She said, "Cass told me you hacked onto her screen name and then called the police to frame her by tracking the screen name."

I almost laughed because I could see the folly in this terrible lie, it made no sense. I couldn't believe people would accept Cass's story without question, and I do not understand how gossip clouds others thought process. People can forget logic because they want to believe some dramatic story just to have something to gossip about. Try telling that to Stella!

ah-ha!

I said to Stella, "Why would I call the police and track something to my own computer? What would be the point?" I didn't let her know Cass's lie had hurt my feelings. Why did Cass feel the need to cover what she did by victimizing me? Didn't she realize her lie would eventually catch up with her? Apparently not!

Stella looked at me and all of a sudden, a wave of understanding washed over her face.

"So you didn't," she asked.

"No," I said and she realized Cass was lying and wanted to know what had really happened.

I told her, "It was Cass's business." No need to make Cass feel worse and create more harsh feelings. She is obviously embarrassed and feeling insecure if she needs to try and ruin my life by spreading terrible rumors.

gossip
gossip

After lunch, some of the gossiping stopped and Cass's smirks turned to glares. It turns out, Alana had booted her from our lunch table and Ash and Nancy now thought Cass was mean.

Later, I asked Alana why she had booted Cass out.

She said, "Cass was slandering your name Dorie."

Part of me was overjoyed this happened, but the other part felt guilty. It's not right to kick somebody out. That's just mean and it's something The Populars would do, not us, the Uber Dubers. If Cass had just said, I'm sorry and thanks for caring, we would still be friends. Instead, she turned on me because she was embarrassed. It hurts my feelings to think a good deed went so wrong. Ours was a special friendship and I wish I could make things better. I never thought she was like this, but maybe I wasn't looking close enough.

Diary, some people in life aren't always what they appear to be. In addition, I must remember even though this exploded in my face, I did the right thing and in the long run, I possibly saved a life. Sometimes, people just don't want to see the truth.

Dorie xoxo ♡ ♡ ♡ ♡ ♡ ♡ ♡ ♡♡

DORIE'S TWO CENTS *FOR SURVIVING AND UNDERSTANDING WHAT GOSSIP CAN DO*

remember when you gossip

Gossiping is destructive. It has the potential to ruin someone's school year. We all know this, so why do we gossip? Is it because we're bored and we have nothing better to do? Maybe it's the satisfaction of falsely inflating your ego at the expense of the victim. We all have been victims and we all have gossiped. Don't deny it because you know you have. Whether it is the snide remark about a person's outfit or a misinformed opinion, we haven't worried about the other person's feelings. We have been there and we are still willing to put some other person through the same amount of pain we went through.

In the last year, I have thought deeply about these things and realized gossiping is not right and it is destructive. Who cares if it's part of our sleepover traditions, because it's wrong and everyone knows it. Instead of ripping each other apart, we need to band together and build each other up. We are alike because we all have feelings. If you know you will hurt someone with gossip, why do you do it? Hurting people is unacceptable and it must be stopped.

Try to make a pact with yourself, I did and it made me a better person. Try to say on Mondays, Wednesdays, and Saturdays, you won't gossip. Every few weeks add another day and soon you will be gossip free. Encourage your friends to do this with you and it will be easier. Also, if you hear someone gossiping about someone else (even if you don't like the person) tell them to stop. You would want them to do the same for you.

REMEMBER THIS

Gossiping is destructive, cruel, and heartless. Not only can it ruin friendships, but it can ruin lives!

Gossip + ♡ = ☮
Let's do it together!
X Xoo Dorie

CHAPTER 14
DOES CASS DESERVE ANOTHER CHANCE?

YES or NO

THE REAL DEAL

interesting

Almost 30% of youth in the United States are estimated to be involved in bullying as either a bully or a target. Bullies have a strong need to dominate others and usually have little empathy. (NYVPRC)

YOUR TWO CENTS

Question 1: What do people usually bully people about?
Response 1: "Whatever they wish they had."
Response 2: "Anything they can find wrong with you."
Question 2: Has a friend been cruel to you, but you forgave them, only to be hurt by them again?
Response 1: "Yes, a good friend of mine had a great party and didn't invite me. Instead, she invited everybody else in the whole grade. I was really sad and depressed and thought I would never forgive her, but I decided to give her a second chance after she apologized and said it would never happen again. I then found out she was talking behind my back and telling all my private secrets and other lies."
Response 2: "Yes, my best friend stole my first boyfriend from me and we didn't talk forever! After a lot of apologies, I finally forgave her and we decided to never let a boy get between us again.
Question 3: Has anyone ever tried to undermine your self-confidence through bulling and how did you handle it?
Response 1: "Yes, this one girl in my grade decided to spread rumors about me so that no one would like me. We used to be best friends too!!!

She became popular and I became the school's biggest loser. It worked, my self-confidence was shattered and I'm still trying to regain it."

Response 2: "No, but it's embarrassing to say that I have done it to others before."

Dear Diary,

Almost everyone at school now believes me and Cass is furious. I think she hates my guts and this really bothers me, but otherwise, things are going well again. Cass is trying to turn Ash and Nancy against me, so I told them to look closely at the whole story before making judgments. I get so annoyed with their whining and lack of backbone when confronted with problems. I explained they need to make their own decisions in life and not believe everything they hear. It's not always a good idea to agree with the majority; you are entitled to your own opinions.

Of course, there is a time when you shouldn't voice your opinions so loudly, but you can have your own ideas. Ash and Nancy are becoming "not so innocent bystanders" and frankly, it's annoying me. When I see something wrong happening, I try to make things right. I will try to be more understanding with Ash and Nancy. I need to realize not everybody is like me and I should focus on the good traits they have, instead of the bad. Diary, this can be difficult at times, but I will try and do a better job.

Dorie

Dear Diary,

Cass wants to hang out with us again. I'm wary and Alana and I do not think it's a good idea because we cannot trust her after what has happened. If she's not honest with us (her supposedly best friends) what is she saying to others? But she has no other friends and I feel so bad for her. I know I shouldn't let her in close proximity because of how much she hurt me last time. What kind of person turns on somebody else after years of friendship? Maybe we weren't real friends to begin with?

123

Luna is talking on the phone so I can't use it. I want to talk with Alana about this, but of course loony Luna is hogging the phone and has a hard time understanding the concept of sharing. I think I will follow her around until she hangs up. Hope it works!

Dorie   Loads of love!

Dear Diary,

Since my life is becoming better, I'm able to realize I have a truly annoying younger sibling and I'm sure she doesn't think much better of me. At least during my crisis, she decided to give me a break and not bug me as much. This morning she made it to the shower before me and let me just say, I might as well give up the line to the bathroom (even though I am the line). Thank goodness my brothers are on the opposite side of the country at college!

Luna took all morning to primp, so I had to go to school without a shower and I felt quite stinky. Well, not completely stinky. I did have some body spray, which I applied in ample amounts, and I ended up smelling like a sour apple. People were sniffing me all day! I don't think guys are attracted to sour apple though, I think they would prefer just out of the shower fresh. Cass sat with us at lunch again and I didn't kick her out because I didn't want to be mean. I didn't feel very comfortable because I'm still not sure if I can trust her. I have heard a leopard never changes its spots, but Cass deserves another chance, doesn't she?

Dorie   right!?????!!

Dear Diary,

I think Cass has finally realized I was just trying to help her and keep her safe. I also think I misjudged her by thinking she wanted to get close again for personal gain or some kind of revenge. Since I have my group of friends back together, I realize I have learned a lot about relationships this school year. Diary, I'm really proud of myself.

Dorie   xoxo ♡ - ♡ ♡

DORIE'S TWO CENTS *FOR SURVIVING BEING AN EASY TARGET*

I'm sure you have seen at least one movie with extremely cruel "mean girls" and these characters are always hurting others, and this seems to give them some sort of satisfaction. It can be like this in real life and I am positive that you know a bully. They could pick on anything from your looks, clothes, grades, family's lifestyle or religion. You may think, "Why pick on me, there's a whole school." It is normal to have these feelings of frustration and you may be unaware you could look like an "easy target" for bullies. It's not right, but often it happens. Below I have described an easy target. If you match up with a lot of these, then you may be an easy target for bullying.

you're not alone.

EASY TARGET:

1. You wouldn't be the one who walks with your head held high in the hallway filled with self-confidence. Instead you look at the floor, afraid to make eye-contact with others.
2. When someone makes fun of you, you don't do anything. You just hang your head and walk away.
3. You have been told more than once, "Get a back bone!"
4. If someone tells you that you need to change something about yourself, you do, without question.
5. You usually let the crowd decide for you because you are afraid to give an opinion.

If you can relate to any of these, there may be an easy explanation why you are an easy target, but don't worry I'm here to help. Let me give you some suggestions to help with the problem. You need to show you are confident and you won't allow others to hurt you. Next time someone starts to bully you, look them straight in the eye and calmly, but firmly say, "Stop. I don't like that." Then walk off with the most confident attitude possible. When you say, "Stop, I don't like that." Your voice needs to show no emotion because you don't want to let the bully see you upset. They want you to be angry or sad and if you show no emotion, but say how you feel, they will be confused. Walking away confidently and calmly shows everyone - no one can mess with you. If you don't like what someone is doing to you, remember, you have the right to say, "Please stop." It is your life and you cannot just sit there waiting for some unknown person to come save you. Most of the time, you need to save yourself.

are an you an easy target? yes! ↓ then do this!

You may be reading this and saying, "I'm not lacking in confidence and I don't have any of the characteristics listed above." This is very possible because many times bullies don't like confident people because bullies always bully because they are insecure. When a person is truly confident, they do not need to hurt others. Bullies also know a confident person will stand up to them, so they often try to destroy another's confidence through harsh words, gossip or physical violence. Any type of destructive behavior they may use, so sometimes it's best to walk away (if you can) and find help. What you need to do, if you feel threatened or bullied, is to keep your confidence intact by asking a trusted adult to become involved. Sometimes, these things can get out of hand and there is never anything wrong with asking for help.

REMEMBER THIS!

Adults do help, so never be afraid to ask for help. Their experience in life helps them see problems more clearly. It is important to build

your confidence and self-esteem; never allow anyone to destroy it! We all are special!!

Confidence Rules!

CHAPTER 15
YOU DON'T HAVE TO BE
IN THE "IT CLIQUE" TO HAVE
A GOOD TIME HANGING WITH FRIENDS.

THE REAL DEAL

A girl who is seen as likable and popular may actually be excluded from belonging to a clique. That's because her personality or confidence may pose a threat to the leaders. She may not be a good follower. Clique members may deliberately exclude her in an attempt to take away her perceived power. (kidshealth.org)

this explains so much!

YOUR TWO CENTS

Question: Do you have an "it clique" at your school? Are they mean or nice? Are you part of it? Do you want to be part of it? If you do want to be part of it, why? Do other people want to be part of it, why?

Response 1: "If I was not in my current clique, I would probably like to be in 'The Clique'...but I do not think that will ever be possible. I don't know what makes 'The Clique' so popular and why everyone wants to be like them. I would definitely say the meanest clique in school is the clique I am currently in. I know, shocking! Well I only think this because I hang out with the clique all the time and I am there when all the mean things happen to one another. I am not in any other cliques, so I do not hear whether people are mean to each other or not. The Nerd Clique definitely does not affect my clique, they are just individuals, but of course smart! However, 'The Clique' affects my clique a lot because of envy. Everyone is jealous of how popular and glamorous 'The Clique' appears and wishes they were like them. Most importantly, the people in my clique envy how all the guys some how only like the girls in 'The Clique.'"

Response 2: "There are the 'cool/popular girls' who I do not find cool at all. Some of them are my friends and I like to hang out with them in small groups or individually, but when they are all together...I actually feel intimidated by them (and I'm not the kind of person who people view as 'intimidated' very often). My best friend and I sort of used to be part of the 'popular group' until we realized how awful they were because they gossiped so much. Now we rely on each other and hang out with pretty much anyone"

Dear Diary,

I have decided I completely forgive Cass for how she hurt me after I tried to help her. After all, she must have been feeling a little lost, but a little voice inside my head tells me to be wary. I'm ignoring it; what does that inner voice know anyway! It's nice to have the whole gang, Alana, Cass, Ash and Nancy, back together again. I'm completely enjoying myself. There is a big dance coming up and Mom said she will drive us if I let Luna and her friends also carpool. Blah!!! It's worth it; I hope. Diary, Luna can be so embarrassing!

Who listens to the inner voice anyways!

Luna

blah!

Dorie

Dear Diary,

Tomorrow the gang and I are going outfit shopping. I might have to ask for a little money from Mom. I spent my money on a really cute purse. Oops!

Dorie

129

Dear Diary,

Outfit shopping was very stressful. Nothing was really in my twenty dollar budget. Wow, inflation! I bought a cute pair of undies and a matching bra. At least if I don't look good on the outside, I'll feel good on the inside. Not that I want any Peeping Toms looking at my undergarments and I'm not going to be showing them off!! It's for my own personal satisfaction. I wasn't the only one who had an empty piggy bank. Instead of buying new outfits, everyone is going to bring as much clothing, shoes and accessories they can carry to my house and then we will swap. I cannot wait; it's going to be awesome!

Dorie

Dear Diary,

It's the night before the dance and my phone has been ringing off the hook. The gang and I have been discussing what to bring. Since we can't carry everything, we must make sacrifices. It's so sad. The decisions have been very hard and at one point, I thought Alana might break down in tears. Alana and Cass are in charge of outfit approval, so they have to bring as much clothing as possible. I'm in charge of make-up and hair and it's a good thing we're meeting at my house, because I don't think I have enough bags to carry my make-up and hair supplies. When I was in the middle of organizing my stuff, Luna came into my room.

"What do you want?" I barked. I really didn't want to know; I just wanted to scare her away. I was not to be so lucky.

"Dorie, you should be wary of Cass because I have a bad feeling about this dance," she said. I waved her off.

ring

ring

big hair rules

"Whatever!" I said. What do little sisters know anyway? It was nice she was concerned though, although it was quite surprising.

Dorie

Dorie !

DORIE'S TWO CENTS *FOR SURVIVING THE "IT CLIQUE"*

It seems at every school there is some sort of "it clique." It always appears as if everybody wants to be hanging out with them or be just like them. This "it clique" can be mean or nice. Sometimes we can become so focused on how much we want to be like them or be friends with them, we forget what is really important. I have realized from experience, being in the "it clique" is not always better. With true friends you can be yourself and relax, while sometimes with the "it clique," you have act like someone else to be popular. Sure, it can be fun pretending to be somebody else, but how long could you last? If you are thinking about ditching your true friends for the "it clique," remember your true friends may be hurt and the friendships ruined. It can take years to earn someone's friendship and trust, but just one poor decision can end it. Next time you make a decision regarding the future of a friendship, try and remember how much the friendship has meant to you. Don't be hasty with decisions because they could cost you in the long run. You don't want to be the girl who ditched her true friends for another clique, only to be rejected within a week. Your friends may be hurt and decide your friendship is over and then you will be in a predicament.

read this

REMEMBER THIS!

Think so you don't stink!

One of my favorite phrases! Are you stinky ??

CHAPTER 16
INNER (SMARTER?) DORIE:
"SOMETIMES THINGS
DON'T TURN OUT THE WAY WE PLAN."
OUTER DORIE: "YOU THINK?"

THE REAL DEAL

In a clique, most of the followers cling to the leader not out of true friendship but because they want to keep their position in the group. Clique members often use flattery, humiliation, or rumors to manipulate situations and preserve their status. (kidshealth.org)

YOUR TWO CENTS

Question 1: What would you do if you were trying to join a clique? How far would you go?
Response 1: "I would be nice to them but I wouldn't do anything that would make me feel uncomfortable."
Response 2: "I think I would do almost anything to join the popular people."
Question 2: Have friends ever gossiped at your expense to make themselves look important? How did you feel? *stop if you do!*
Response 1: "Yes, angry!"
Response 2: "One friend does it all the time and I don't know why."

Dear Diary,

über wrong   I really thought tonight at the dance was going to be a good night, but I thought wrong. It started out so well. When the gang and I jumped on the school bus, the Bus Crowd didn't appear very happy so many other people were riding the bus. Luna also had her friends for the dance, so finding a seat was very difficult. Possibly it was because we were not really quiet either, but we were so excited talking about the chances of being asked to dance. Just thinking about a cute guy asking us to dance resulted in the gang falling into a fit of giggles.

When we finally arrived at my house, the bus driver looked very relieved. I really don't blame him because it must have been distracting trying to concentrate on the road, while a bunch of girls laughed hysterically in random outbursts. Cass made a not very nice comment about me to the gang, but I just brushed it aside because it wasn't the time for drama. Looking back, I should have taken this as a sign, but I was too excited. We all rushed to my bedroom with a million and one bags and Luna and her friends ran to hers.

I warned everybody, "If you need to take a shower, do so now or forever hold your peace, because Luna, the bathroom hog, is here." Good thing no one needed a shower because Luna's friends had beaten us to the most coveted room in the house. We all began to organize outfits.

I wore Cass's short jean skirt with little pockets in the front for mints and money. (Mom would never buy me a short jean skirt!) I also wore my own black undershirt and Alana's shirt overtop. It was so cute!!! She may not be seeing this shirt again. It was light yellow with an empire waist, short sleeves and it flowed nicely over my body. It's hard to explain Diary, so I drew a picture. I used my own jewelry with the outfit and I had a lot of beads around my neck (I'll put it that way). I also had quite a few bangles on my arm. *so cute*
Everybody looked pretty similar and we all had the same style skirt, but in different colors. Of course, our hair and make-up looked gorgeous because this was my department.

After a brief inspection to make sure everything was looking good, we headed down stairs to eat piz-za because we can't dance on an empty stomach. Everybody went downstairs before me so I could tidy my room a little more. When I walked out of my room, Luna was coming out of hers and we both looked each other up and down. She looked like she

133

came out of a Tommy Hilfiger Catalog while I looked exactly the opposite. Who would believe we are related? While she walked gracefully down the stairs, I took one step and tumbled all the way down. When I reached the bottom, my skirt had risen up so my new panties were quite visible. (At least they were pretty; pink and green; my favorite colors!) Luna and her friends just stared while the gang and I burst out laughing as they helped me stand up. It was kind of funny, even though my tush didn't take kindly to the fall.

The first half of the dance was really fun and we danced together in a group. Sadly, no one asked me to dance. I wonder if anyone will ever ask me to dance or am I destined to be a solo dancer my whole life? I was having too much fun to worry and I reminded myself, I have my whole life ahead of me to be asked to dance.

By the middle of the dance, a huge group of people had gathered around Cass and she was glowing from their attention. Some of the people I recognized as members of the Almost Populars and even a few from The Populars. Everybody was making astonished faces and a few were even looking in my direction. I saw Nancy and Ash were also with Cass, and I wanted to know what was going on, so I walked over. Once I came close they all stopped talking and just stared at me. A nasty feeling started to build in my stomach and I tried to suppress it by thinking positive thoughts. Maybe she was telling them how I fell down the stairs?

Sadly, I was not to be so lucky. No, I was about to learn the true level of Cass's anger with me and her plan of revenge. I should have seen it coming, but I didn't. I refused to listen to Luna and the little voice inside that said "be careful."

"Hi," I said, "what's going on?"

Everyone just looked at me, but Nancy, Ash, and Cass wouldn't look me in the eye. I knew what this was about, but no, she wouldn't start this gossip again. Not after how nice I have been to her. Why would she do this, for attention?

My worst fears materialized when somebody said, "Uh, oh, I think she's going to call the police on us." They didn't say it in a very pleasant tone either. I walked away and found Alana and she said she was going to join Cass and the others, even though she heard through the fast gossip chain what had just happened.

bad turns to worse

"Do you know what she did?" I said.

"Ya," replied Alana.

"Then why are you going to go support her. You're my best friend!" I shot back

"Gee, Dorie. You don't have to be so sensitive," Alana retorted.

"You pick right now, her or me," I said. I didn't know who she was going to pick, but I thought she would pick me over Cass. After all, we had been friends longer. I was wrong.

Alana looked at me, then at Cass, who was surrounded by the gang and The Popular Clique, and walked away ending our friendship. I stood there in disbelief, so hurt I felt nauseous. Tears burned my eyes and I started to feel dizzy. I had to get away, I had to hide. All of a sudden, Luna burst through the crowd and was at my side with a determined look on her face.

Friends forever ? .

"Come on," she said, "let's get out of here." We exchanged a glance and I was in shock. She was willing to leave her friends and the dance when she was having such a great time - for me. I realized I really am lucky to have Luna because she always comes through for me when I really need her.

"Thanks," was all I could choke out as she led me out of the crowded gym. I could barely see and was sure my mascara was running down my face, but I didn't care. All I wanted to do was leave and go home, so Luna called Mom to pick us up early.

Mom was a bit baffled on the ride home because we were so quiet, but she didn't ask too many questions. I think she knew something was wrong and

we weren't ready to talk about it. Luna was so nice. I couldn't believe how she rescued me. Who would believe with all of our differences, she would be there when I needed her most. I guess family really does matter.

It's late at night, but I can't stop crying. Why did this happen to me?!? I can't believe all of my friends deserted me, especially Alana, and we have been friends for so long. I am confused and angry, why would she do this? I hate her, but at the same time I wish this had never happened. I think my heart has broken into a thousand little pieces. How could I have been so naïve? I should have seen this coming. Luna was right (it takes a lot to admit this) I should have been careful with Cass and not trusted her so blindly. I could have stopped this problem by keeping my distance from Cass, but I didn't, so now I am lying here in my bed friendless. Diary, I don't think I'll ever be happy again.

Dorie

DORIE'S TWO CENTS *FOR SURVIVING LOSING A FRIENDSHIP*

normal feelings

It can be really hard when a friendship has ended, especially when somebody ditches you for another friend who has hurt you. Often, you feel confused, sad and angry, but remember these feelings are normal. It is important you confront and analyze the pain, instead of ignoring and allowing it to grow inside your heart. You may need to talk to a trusted adult about these feelings to understand and move past the pain. If you ignore your feelings, you could feel worse and become depressed. Often, we start feeling sorry for ourselves and wallow in self-pity. We think about how terrible our life is and how we don't deserve what has happened. When this happens, follow the advice below because it has helped me many times when I have been confronted with these feelings.

read

Step one: Stop feeling sorry for yourself and be aware it is normal to feel confused, sad and angry at times, but it serves no purpose to become depressed.

Step two: Follow the "***new girl suggestions***" for making new friends. This can be found in ***Chapter 2*** in ***Dorie's Two Cents***.

Step three: Remember, you are not new to the school and you know many of the students. Also, you don't need to impress anyone, just be yourself—you are "good enough" just as you are and you will find new friends. If someone is cruel or is trying to make you do crazy or embarrassing things to become their friend, walk away and find new friends. Real friends should never embarrass or hurt you.

So true! **Step four:** Remember, you are a good person and it's easy to love you. Relax, be confident and be yourself and you'll have people flocking to you in no time.

REMEMBER THIS!

Real friends make you feel good about being you!

An important lesson for your whole life

137

CHAPTER 17
HOW CAN YOU STAB MY BACK?
YOU WERE SUPPOSED TO
BE WATCHING IT!

THE REAL DEAL

While many people believe that bullies act tough in order to hide feelings of insecurity, in fact, bullies tend to be confident, with high self-esteem. Surprisingly, bullies appear to have little difficulty in making friends. (NYVPRC)

YOUR TWO CENTS

Check Bully Fact Sheet

Question 1: Why do you think bullies bully in general?
Response 1: "Because their insecure."
Response 2: "Because they're bored."
Question 2: Have you ever been backstabbed by a friend or backstabbed a friend? How did you deal with it? Are you still friends?
Response 1: "She made up rumors that my friend and I were saying mean things about each other to her, but we really weren't. No"
Response 2: "I backstabbed a friend and regret it. I miss our friendship."

Dear Diary,

Things just aren't going well. I talked to Alana in private and she was pretty nasty. I told her how I felt about her ditching me and she didn't even apologize!! She just tried to justify her behavior, but everything she said I could counteract. If she had only apologized, I would have immediately forgiven her. I officially have no friends and I never want to go back to school. How can I roam the halls friendless? She hurt my feelings so much and I'm confused because she made it sound like I was the bad one. What should I have done? Stand there at the dance looking like a bimbo head while everyone talked about me? Oh yes, I could have told myself, "La dee da dee da, was that my name I heard?" I don't think so!! We have been friends since second grade!!!! I don't think she has ever made me feel like this before. I trusted Alana and Cass and they just backstabbed me and what about Ash and Nancy? Did our friendship mean nothing?

Dorie

Dear Diary,

School was horrible! People were talking terribly about me and no one would talk to me. Every time I went past Alana, Cass, Ash and Nancy, I could feel their eyes on me as they laughed and whispered quietly back and forth with snide glances my way. The whispering really bugged me because they were supposed to be my friends and I thought they cared about my feelings. I felt alone and helpless, so I kept my eyes glued to the ground and kept walking. I don't know for sure if they were talking about me, but I'm pretty sure they were.

Lunch was really bad because I had no place to sit. Whenever I came towards a table, people would stop talking and just stare at me or they would start whispering. As I came closer to the table, they glared to indicate I was not welcome to sit with them. Since I was hungry and there were no open tables, I went to the bathroom in the east wing of the school. It was closest to my next class and I could just throw the garbage away in the bathroom because I had brought my own lunch (my favorite, turkey sandwich with pickles). Plus, I would avoid passing people in the hallway and save myself from more embarrassment. The bathroom was empty, so I went into the middle stall and sat down. It was really lonely, but at least I didn't have to hear people talking about me or see everyone staring at me. I noticed on the bathroom stall there was a lot of writing and some of it was about me.

x Best Friend.

Diary, I ignored this because of words I won't repeat, but there was one thing which caught my eye. In the bottom left corner of the stall door, somebody had written a question and another had answered.

It said, "What do you most regret?"

Then in the same handwriting Alana uses, it said, "Leaving my best friend."

When I saw this, I broke down into tears. If this really was Alana and she felt this way, why didn't she do something to save our friendship? I don't understand why people act this way. Why does Alana talk badly about me and why do people believe her? Why is she ruining my life and reputation? I don't understand what is wrong with people!!! I'm not a bad person!! Why is it that all the nice people get made fun of? Better yet, why do people even make fun of others? Things just don't add up.

Dorie

Dear Diary,

I feel like this is all a game and you have to play your cards right, one wrong move and you are done; game's over. The rules change daily and for different situations. I can't understand the rules, never mind following them, and I don't think I should have to play a game with my best friends; it's just not right! Furthermore, if you let your guard down, you could lose track of the game and play a losing card. Before you even understand the rules, the game is over. It's like one big poker game, trading one card for another and trying to call each others bluff. One big circle that goes around and around and around without an end. Diary, I think I've lost the game, but even if I haven't will it ever stop? I have decided I don't like poker!

Dorie

DORIE'S TWO CENTS *FOR SURVIVING BEING BACKSTABBED*

Being backstabbed and betrayed by a close friend can be a very stressful and hurtful experience. Many times it is unexpected and we are completely unprepared. Follow a few of these ideas to deal with the problem, but remember, results may vary depending on the situation.

They help!

SUGGESTIONS FOR SURVIVING BACKSTABBING:

1. Confront your friend in calm manner. Tell her how it made you feel without sounding accusatory. If your friend apologizes sincerely and has never hurt you like this before, you could think about giving her/him another chance at friendship. If she/he has done this before or doesn't apologize, then I would highly consider evaluating your friendship. Is it really a healthy relationship?

2. If you decide it isn't a healthy relationship you should follow the *"new girl suggestions"* found in ***Dorie's Two Cents*** in ***Chapter 2*** because it may be time to branch out and meet some new people. The best place to meet new people is in the lunch room, in class, or in the hallways, but you may even find friends outside of your school. Keep your eyes open and be positive!

REMEMBER THIS!

There is probably someone experiencing the same feelings of betrayal so reach out and look for friendships in new places in and outside of school. You may be pleasantly surprised to discover new and enjoyable friendships!

Look for new friends in new places and smile! ☺

CHAPTER 18
LUNA, HELPFUL?
THE WORLD MUST HAVE
TURNED UPSIDE DOWN!

THE REAL DEAL

Tell your parents or other trusted adults if you are bullied. They can help stop the bullying. If you are bullied at school, tell your teacher, school counselor or principal. Telling is not tattling. (HRSA)

YOUR TWO CENTS

Question 1: If you have ever been bullied did you tell anybody or keep quiet?
Response 1: "At first I didn't tell anybody because I thought it would make the problem worse. I realized that was not so when I got an adult involved."
Response 2: "I did and I'm glad. Now I don't feel so alone."

Dear Diary,

The last few days have been torture. I'm trying to act like nothing is wrong so my family won't realize I'm having problems at school. My mom has already started asking questions, and I just side step all of them, but Luna was not so easily fooled. After all, she does go to the same school and she saw what happened at the dance. When I was lying on my bed with my music turned up really high, she came in and started talking. At first, I thought it was to yell at me for having my music on so loud. I was ready for her to say something extremely rude and I was starting to think of comebacks, then she opened her mouth and surprised me.

"I know what's going on in school. Are you ok?" she asked.

"I'm fine," I answered.

"No you're not, stop lying to me!" Luna demanded.

This was how our conversation started and I had no idea Luna even cared about my feelings or could be so sensitive. It made me feel good because I realized no matter what happens at school, my family will always be here for me. She just listened as I laid my head on a pillow and cried and talked. It was really comforting to get it all off my chest and tell somebody, I feel a lot better now and I don't feel so alone. I have decided, tomorrow night I'm going to come up with a plan on how to overcome my negative feelings and deal with my problems at school.

Dorie

Dear Diary,

Today was once again, not a great day because no one talked to me and I ate my lunch alone in the bathroom. While I seem to get less and less popular, Alana and Cass are getting more popular and sometimes they hang out with The Populars. They gained their popularity by gossiping about me. Is that how little our friendship meant; could it be so easily pawned away for five minutes of fame? Don't they realize The Populars only want their gossip, not their friendship? Things need to change, so I have made my survival plan and the ideas come straight from my Totally Notably. I will do one or two things every day and keep the plan going until things change for the better at school.

SURVIVAL PLAN:

1. Stop feeling sorry for myself.

2. Try and meet new people everyday.
3. Start realizing that if people talk like this about me, they are most likely talking in this manner about everyone.
4. Stop eating lunch in the bathroom and sit at a random table in the lunch room with the kindest looking people.

I'm not sure how this will work, but it's worth a shot. The only way I'll get through this is to stop caring what other people think about me and to start caring about what I think about myself. It is easier said than done because no matter what I try, think or do, the gossip always remains just a tiny bit in my brain. I am going to try as hard as I can to forget the past and move forward.

Dorie   ♡ 🎀 x x o o

DORIE'S TWO CENTS *FOR SURVIVING BULLYING AND WHEN TO KNOW IT'S TIME TO ASK FOR HELP*

→ must learn

When you are bullied it's not a pleasant experience and sometimes you may feel threatened or scared. If this happens, you should never hesitate to tell someone and ask for help. Sometimes, just sharing your story will help you feel better inside and possibly, another person could provide a new outlook on the situation and have answers to ensure your safety. Also, you could receive advice you would have never considered and it may help solve the problem. When you are scared or feel threatened, you NEED to leave and speak with a trusted adult because things can become dangerous and the problem could escalate before you even know it. We've all seen the violent videos in the news of people being viciously attacked. You don't want to be the next victim! Asking for help could keep you safe and possibly make the situation better.

Please Do!

REMEMBER THIS!

It's your choice; if you don't feel comfortable with people or situations then leave. Please make the smart choice and be safe!

Always respect yourself
and be safe!
        make smart choices.
    xxoo Dorie

CHAPTER 19
MY LAUGHTER? WHAT A SURPRISE!

THE REAL DEAL

helpful What should you do if you're bullied? Try not to show anger or fear. Students who bully like to see that they can upset you. Use humor if this is easy for you to do. (For example, if a student makes fun of your clothing, laugh and say, "Yeah, I think this shirt is kind of funny-looking too.") (HRSA)

YOUR TWO CENTS

Question 1: If you are not part of a clique, why aren't you? Have you ever tried to join a clique? What happened when you tried to join a clique?
Response 1: "I'm not because I don't like the idea of cliques. I have a lot of friends, but not in one clique."
Question 2: What would you do if a clique was bullying you?
Response 1: "If a clique was bullying me, I would try to stay away from them."
Response 2: "I would talk to my parents and in school pretend the bullying wasn't bothering me."

Dear Diary,

Today at lunch I sat with the Smarty Pants Clique. They weren't really thrilled, but at least they were nice to me. I listened to their conversation and couldn't help but steal a glance at my old table. I had never seen it so full! My heart started to ache and I felt grief overwhelm me. The gang was laughing and having the time of their lives, *without* me. The table not only had Alana, Ash, Nancy and Cass, but a bunch of guys and girls from the Almost Popular Clique and Wanna Be Popular

Stitches

146

Clique. I couldn't help but think, they traded me for popularity! What type of friends would do this?

I thanked the Smarty Pants for letting me sit with them and stood up to put my tray away and use the restroom. As I passed my old table, one of the guys sitting there stood up and started walking towards me. I could hear giggles and people saying, "Don't," but it was too late and he was standing right next to me.

My stomach began to churn because I didn't want another incident to provide additional negative gossip. I could see everybody's eyes in the lunchroom watching me. It was extremely unnerving!!!

The guy said, "Hi," and then said, "you need to apologize for what you did to Cass and Alana."

I looked at him and then at Alana and Cass who were giggling. Girls, who were my former best friends, couldn't even say it to my face so they had to have someone else do it. I looked back at him. I couldn't help but think it was rather pathetic! This guy, with a squeaky voice and a whopping six inches shorter than me, thought he was going to make me say sorry for doing the right thing. All of a sudden, I laughed. At first it was somewhat quiet, but then it turned into a loud, high pitched, hysterical laugh and I didn't care. Some people stopped eating and stared at this strange scene. A boy saying something to a girl, with all of his friends watching and looking confused, and the girl, who clearly had been ostracized, was laughing at the very thing that was supposed to make her cry. I left him standing there dumbfounded and walked slowly to the bathroom, still shivering with giggles. For the first time, I wasn't crying because I was sad; it was because I was laughing!

For the rest of the day, every time I passed my old gang I wasn't met by the usual giggles and stares, but by really confused faces. I came home today feeling better than ever before. Diary, want to know the funniest thing? Luna said when I left the lunch room people just stared at Cass and the other people at the lunch table and no one knew what to say. For the first time ever, the lunchroom was speechless!

Dorie *Don't mess — Dorie*

DORIE'S TWO CENTS *FOR SURVIVING AND SURPRISING OTHERS*

good plan → Many people expect a specific reaction from certain actions, but they are never prepared and are often startled when you don't react the way they had expected. If a clique is bullying you, it is often best to act the opposite way they expect; try using laughter. Think about it, there is a whole group of people making fun of you, and clearly they are insecure if they need to have a group. They are trying to encourage one person in their group to do something extremely cruel and they anticipate you will become upset. Try the laughter approach and see if it eases the tension and diffuses the situation. Look at them, start laughing and walk away. Possibly, they won't bully you anytime soon because by using laughter, you leave them looking like a fool.

REMEMBER THIS!

No one messes with you unless you allow it!

So don't allow it...ever!
Dorie ♥

CHAPTER 20
NEW FRIENDS IN NEW PLACES!

THE REAL DEAL

Victims of bullying experience loneliness and report having trouble making social and emotional adjustments, difficulty making friends, and poor relationships with classmates. (U.S. Dept. of Justice)

YOUR TWO CENTS

try to help!

Question: If you saw someone sitting alone at lunch, would you invite them to sit with you even if your friends might not approve?
Response 1: "I would try, but if my friends where rude or mean I would forget it."
Response 2: "No, I would be too afraid of what my friends would say."

Dear Diary,

I'm starting to feel like my old self again, even if I am a loner. I do miss Alana, a lot, and it's so weird not hanging out or speaking with her. We've been friends for such a long time and I often wonder if she misses me as well. I can't help but sometimes wish I was walking down the hall with her, instead of by myself. Maybe someday we'll be friends again, but I don't know if I'll want her friendship because: how can it be the same? Today, I saw Cass, Nancy, Ash and their new found friends making fun of me and I heard Alana tell them to knock it off. Does this mean she feels the same way; does she miss me too? I wonder if I'll ever know.

Dorie   XO XOXO XO

Dear Diary,

Today I was hanging out with some new people. Their names are Hope, Angie and Cathy and they're really nice. When I was trying to find a place to sit at lunch, they called out and asked if I would sit with them. It felt really good some-one actually wanted my company, and I felt this was a good start. I laughed really hard during lunch because they had a great sense of humor. It is kind of like my sense of humor (which no one seems to understand) and I think they have a lot of friends. Hope, Angie and Cathy are what we call "Floaters" in our school and everyone likes them. They don't belong to a particular clique and are dictionary definition popular because they are con-fident and nice to everyone. They don't worry about what others say or think of them.

Hope has long black hair which reaches her butt and she looks like she walked out of an advertisement from the sixties (she wears it well). She is so nice and is really into recy-cling and saving the planet. She wears almost all organic clothing and she is writing a petition to the mayor to stop the digging up of the town park to build a dump. I really admire her. Angie has curly brown hair that reaches the middle of her back. She and Cathy wear clothes from stores like Hollister and American Eagle. Angie is so funny and there is no doubt in my mind when she grows up, she will be a comedian. Cathy is probably the smartest girl I know and she also has blond hair and is very (how shall I say this) voluptuously curvy. Some people say she is dumb (she can act like it) but once you get to know her you realize she earns straight A's for a reason!

Diary, I'm really glad I met these girls. I hope we be-come better friends because when I'm with them, I'm not afraid to be myself.

Dorie

Finally !!

Dear Diary,

There is a school play coming up soon and one of the members of the Drama Club wrote it. Cathy wants to try out, but she is really nervous of making a fool of herself.

"That," I told her, "is a ridiculous notion."

She is such an amazing actress; she could make the strictest teacher believe her tear filled story about why she couldn't do her homework. Angie, Hope and I are not going to let her back out and we said, "If you try to back out, we will stand in the back of the theater during the auditions (which she will go to) and loudly pretend to be Team Cathy Cheerleaders." I think we scared her out of skipping the auditions. Her only big competition is Stella, but I think everybody, including the drama teacher, is ready for a new star.

Dorie

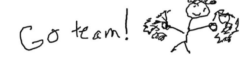

Go team!

DORIE'S TWO CENTS *ON SURVIVING NOT SITTING ALONE*

Sitting alone is not fun. If you have been the one sitting alone, I'm sure you understand the anxiety. It may seem easier to pretend you don't see the person all alone and you may say, "Why not let someone else invite the person to come and sit with them." It really is not right to think this way because nobody else may end up helping the person by inviting the person to sit. When we see someone looking lost, confused or alone, we should ask if they need help or invite them to join us. Helping others may seem like a burden, but being kind will become easier with practice. You may be thinking, "I'd love to invite someone to sit with me, but my friends may not approve." If they are your real friends,

stress

Hello, Why not?

they won't become too upset if you invite someone new to join your group.

REMEMBER THIS!

If your friends do freak out then maybe they need a news flash: it's not nice to exclude people! Come on, we learned this one in kindergarten.

do we really need to
go back there?

CHAPTER 21
EVERYBODY DESERVES TO WIN,
IF YOU DON'T, STEP DOWN GRACEFULLY.

THE REAL DEAL

Being bullied is not your fault, and it is wrong. No matter what you say, how you look, or what you believe, nothing gives anyone else the right to make fun of or hurt you. (NCVC)

YOUR TWO CENTS

look at other survey

Question 1: Do you think jealousy plays a big part in bullying?
Response 1: "Yes, often because of how you look."
Response 2: "I think it may play a part, but how big? I don't know."
Question 2: Have you ever behaved badly towards someone else because you were jealous?
Response 1: "Yes, I spread terrible rumors."
Response 2: "I made my other friends quit talking to the person. I was afraid they would like her better than me."

Dear Diary,

You know how Stella always gets the lead role in plays? Cathy beat her!!!! Stella was so upset she was crying in the bathroom and the Drama Club was glaring at Cathy the whole day! It was priceless because for the first time, Stella didn't get what she wanted and boy; she was not a graceful loser! I do feel bad for her because usually she has the star role, so it must be such a shock, but I don't understand why Stella is so upset because she stars in plays outside of school all the time. It's time to share the stage and spotlight. You can't win everything and if you do, there would be no

a star is born

153

fun in trying. Hope, Angie and I are going together to see Cathy in the play. I can't wait!!

Dorie

ya, ya, yay yay!

Dear Diary,

Stella was extremely cruel today! She spread a terrible rumor about Cathy only receiving the lead role because her parents know the drama teacher really well. How terrible is that? Stella is officially a sore loser. Can't she take the supporting role with grace? Many people would love to have her role and some people didn't even receive a part in the play. Nobody believes her rumor, and it is quite easy to tell she only made it up because she was jealous. I wish people would have thought this way when there were rumors about me. Oh well, can't dwell on the past; I can only move forward.

tsk, tsk.

Dorie

DORIE'S TWO CENTS *FOR SURVIVING ENVY AND JEALOUSY*

At times, it is normal to want something someone else possesses. Everybody has felt this way, and if not, you certainly are not human. There are two different types of wanting; envy and jealousy and there is a big difference between the two. *know the difference!* When you are envious of someone you are happy for the person, although you would love to have the quality, characteristic or other attribute they possess. If you are jealous of someone, then you become upset because you don't have the quality, characteristic or other attribute they possess. Also, jealousy often leads people to do negative things, such as spreading rumors or even stealing.

When Cathy received the lead role and Stella didn't; Stella became jealous. Instead of being happy for Cathy's success, Stella became mean because she wanted the role. Stella spread rumors to try and make herself feel better. Often, when people are jealous of someone they become a bully because it is their way of punishing the person for having something they want. It's not right and if you are doing this, you should stop. Next time you feel the green monster of jealousy creeping up inside of you; try to feel happy for the person, instead of being cruel. At first it may be hard, but if you practice it will come easier.

Not Good!!!

REMEMBER THIS!

You are not going to win everything in life, and you need to learn how to be a gracious loser.

Be happy for others! ♥

CHAPTER 22
HAVING FUN BEING THE UNPOPULAR, SOMETIMES DORKY—ME.

THE REAL DEAL

Want to know the real secret to being popular and having friends? Be a good friend to yourself. Being a friend means being respectful, fair, interested, trustworthy, honest, caring, and kind. (kidshealth.org)

YOUR TWO CENTS

look it up in the dictionary

Question 1: How would you describe the word popular?
Response 1: "Someone who is supposed to be nice but is actually sometimes really mean."
Response 2: "Someone well liked and accepted."
Question 2: Is there a group(s) in your school that is popular? Why are they popular?
Response 1: "They think they are so cool and can do anything they want, but if you actually have the guts to ask other people what they think about their behavior, you realize the only people who like the popular group are themselves!!"
Response 2: "There is a popular group in my school and they are popular because they are really nice to everyone."

Dear Diary,

I'm really sorry I haven't written in a while. We're coming to the end of the school year and things have been a bit hectic, so many tests and other things have kept me busy. When I finally go to bed, I am too exhausted to write. Cathy was great in the play and she definitely deserved the part; she blew everybody's socks off. She was so dramatic I think I even saw a few people with tears in their eyes.

We waved to her so she would know we were there. It was so much fun. At one point, we were making faces at her and she looked like she was going to laugh. The three of us had to look away so we wouldn't be the cause of her messing up her lines, which she never did.

 I would never have guessed I could enjoy myself so much with these friends because I always thought they weren't my type. My mom says, "Everything happens for a reason," and I think she's right. If Alana and I hadn't fought, I would have never met new friends. That's something to think about. Also, I need to remember not to say, "Oh, I wouldn't like someone like that, they're not my type of friend," before I know them. Diary, you never know if you will like a person until you give them a chance.

Dorie

Dear Diary,

There is only one week of school left. I have good grades and I'm feeling much better about my life and myself. My new friends are great! We are really getting to know each other and we have such a blast together. We may not be really close now, but who knows, by next year we could be best friends. All I know is when I hang out with them, I feel good about myself and there are no games. I know Alana and I will mend broken bridges, but for now it feels good to have expanded my horizon by making new friendships. Diary, best of all, I'm FINALLY not the school gossip!!!!!

Dorie

I DID IT!

DORIE'S TWO CENTS *ON SURVIVING AND ACCEPTING BEING WITH PEOPLE WHO MAKE YOU FEEL GOOD; POPULAR OR NOT*

true

Throughout the school year, I've realized something. Calling someone popular is really an opinion and in the end it really doesn't matter. Popular really means generally liked and this would be Hope, Angie, and Cathy. The term "popular" in a movie like *Mean Girls*, would be The Populars in my school. If I was hanging out with The Populars, would I be having so much fun? We really need to think about why we actually like people. Most people are afraid of The Populars and speaking out against them? Why? It's just easier to tag along? To really achieve the feeling of satisfaction in life you need to relax and just be yourself. If the people you hang out with don't like the real you, they probably just like your mask. People, who are going to treat you well, will like you for who you are. No matter how weird you think the "real you" is, don't forget to let it shine.

REMEMBER THIS!

The "real you" is inside and won't be happy until it takes the floor and shines!

→ main point

CHAPTER 23
I LOVE A HAPPY ENDING!

THE REAL DEAL

What can you do to lend a hand? Say kind words to the child who is being bullied, such as "I'm sorry about what happened," and "I don't like it!" Be a friend. Invite that student to do things with you, such as sit together at lunch or work together on a project. EVERYONE NEEDS A FRIEND! (HRSA) *It's true!*

YOUR TWO CENTS

Question: Now is your time to speak up, so if you want to say something, write it down.
Response: "People should stop bullying, start being nicer, and start caring more about other people's feelings. BE NICE!"

Dear Diary,

It is finally the end of the school year and what a year it has been! At one point, I really didn't think I could survive the bullying and gossiping, but I did and I'm really proud of myself! I made some great new friends and I found out I really like me, just as I am. Also, I discovered that Luna was my friend besides being my sister. Who knew she could be so nice (at times)? I tried to do the right thing and be a good friend and I know it will pay off with friendships next year. Some things just take time. I'm so excited for summer! Our family will go to our lake cottage for the whole vacation and I will also go to camp for two weeks. Maybe I will make new friends? For now, I can just hope for the best and wonder what adventures the summer will have

in store for me. Diary, of course you'll be the first to know!

Dorie

DORIE'S TWO CENTS *ON SURVIVING A HAPPY ENDING*

After a long year, it is good to look back and reflect. Many things have gone wrong and many things have gone well. It is important we learn from our mistakes and move on in life. We cannot dwell on the past and keep old grudges, nor can we feel upset with ourselves for making a mistake. Let go; forgive and forget, then move on because this is the key and the answer to happiness in life. Instead of thinking how horrific an experience was, look back on it and think about all of the lessons you have learned. My year was full of a lot of drama, but I learned a lot about myself and my friends. I met new people because I branched out and welcomed new friendships. Best of all, I have achieved an inner peace because I feel good about being Dorie Witt. Think about the negative things that have happened to you, and if you remove yourself from the incident, it will be easier to see why it happened and what you have learned. Let go of old harsh feelings and you too will find inner peace. Inner peace is nothing more than liking yourself for who you are and remember, you are special just the way you are!

REMEMBER THIS!

The best friend you will ever have is yourself so be kind and expect life to be a bumpy road at times. All will work out if you give it time, respect yourself and others, be kind and never give up. Please remember, EVERYONE NEEDS A FRIEND!

Love you,

Dorie!!

Please visit me at doriewitt.com or email me at <u>dorie@doriewitt.com</u>.

I would love to hear from you!!

SOURCES CONSULTED

U.S. Department of Health and Human Services, Health Resources and Service Administration (HRSA); *Stop Bullying Now*

National Youth Violence Prevention Resource Center (NYVPRC); *Bullying Facts and Statistics,* (safeyouth.org)

United States Department of Health and Human Resources— Substance Abuse and Mental Health Services Administration, National Mental Health Information Center (SAMHSA); *Bullying is Not a Fact of Life; Eating Disorders*

National Crime Prevention Council (NCPC); *Bullying*

The National Crime for Victims of Crime (NCVC); *Teen Tools, Help for Teenage Victims of Crime*

Hinduja, S. and Patchin, J.W. (2005). *Research Summary: Cyberbullying Offending.* Preliminary findings from an online survey of Internet-using adolescents (www.cyberbullying.us)

About.com, Inc., a part of the New York Times Company; *The Difference Between Negative and Positive Peer Pressure.* (www.about.com)

The National Center for Missing and Exploited Children (NCMEC); *Teen Internet Safety Study*

Kids Health: *Coping With Cliques,* (kidshealth.org)

U.S. Department of Justice, Office of Justice Programs, Office of Juvenile Justice and Delinquency Prevention; *Addressing the Problem of Juvenile Bullying*

National Institute of Mental Health (NIMH); *Eating Disorders*

National Eating Disorders Association,; *What Should I Say? Tips for Talking to a Friend Who May Be Struggling With an Eating Disorder,* (www.NationalEating Disorders.org)

BULLYING FACT SHEET

Please copy this and feel free to share it with all of your friends. Educate others so we can put a stop to bullying!

FACT:

Almost 30% of youth in the United States (or over 5.7 million) are estimated to be involved in bullying as either a bully, a target of bullying, or both. In a recent national survey of students in grades 6-10, 13% reported bullying others, 11% reported being a target of bullies, and another 6% said that they bullied others and were bullied themselves. (NYVPRC)

WHAT IS BULLYING?

Bullying is intentional aggressive behavior that involves an imbalance of power or strength. It is typically repeated over, and over again. On many occasions, the children have little means of defending themselves. Bullying can take many forms such as verbal and physical bullying, nonverbal bullying i.e., emotional bullying or cyber bullying. Below are definitions of these types of bullying.

DEFINITIONS OF BULLYING:

Verbal bullying: example; teasing, name-calling, spreading rumors. This can be to the person's face or behind their back. This is called harassment and it is against the law.

Physical bullying: example; hitting, punching, tripping, pushing. Any physical action that injures or harms another person. This is called assault and battery and it is against the law.

Nonverbal/emotional bullying: example; intimidation, using gestures, social exclusion. This can also be interpreted as harassment which is against the law.

Cyber bullying: a term used to describe the use of the Internet, cell phones, or other technology to send or post text or images intended to hurt or embarrass another person. It can occur anywhere online, including Internet web sites, chat rooms, anonymous electric bulletin boards, instant messaging, and other web devices. Statements amounting to cyber bullying do not have to be sent directly to the victim. Indirect activities, such as posting a rumor on a public message board, can also be acts of cyber bullying.

WHO BULLIES? WHO IS A BULLY?

Anyone can be a bully, it doesn't matter their ethnic background, or lifestyle. Usually, bullies have been shown to have average or above average self esteem. In fact, contrary to popular belief, they usually have a large peer group that supports a pro-violence attitude and the activities the bully is engaging in.

COMMON CHARACTERISTICS OF A BULLY INCLUDE:

- Impulsive
- Hotheaded
- Dominant
- Easily frustrated
- Lack empathy
- Difficulty following the rules
- View violence in a positive way

Often, children who bully tend to get in trouble more and to dislike or do poorly in school than teens who do not bully others. Also, children and teens who come from homes where parents do not provide a lot of emotional support and fail to monitor their activities are often bullies. Also, if a parents discipline style is extremely permissive or excessively harsh it can increase the risk of the child or teen being a bully. In a study, 60% of those characterized as bullies in grades 6-9 had a least one criminal conviction by the age of 24! Chronic bullies seem to maintain habits into adulthood. (NCPC)

AM I A BULLY?

You are a bully if you partake or watch without stopping any form of bullying stated in the section "what is bullying".

Also, in a study done in urban elementary schools, "40% of the teachers admitted to bullying students and 3% said frequently." (HRSA)

WHO IS BULLIED?

- In a national survey conducted on teens 12 to 17 years old by the National Mental Health Association (SAMHSA), 78% of kids reported that gay or thought to be gay teens are teased and bullied in their schools or communities. Furthermore, 93% hear derogatory words about sexual orientation.
- In a study of children ages 11-16, researchers found that obese or overweight children were more likely to be teased or bullied than normal weight peers. (HRSA)
- Children with some sort of paralysis are more likely than other kids their age to be victimized by peers, to be rated less popular by their peers, and to have less friends than other children. (HRSA)
- Children who have diabetes and are dependent on insulin may be especially vulnerable to peer bullying. (HRSA)
- In a study, 83% of adults who had problems with stammering as children said that they were teased or bullied; 71% said every week. (HRSA)

- Children with disabilities or special needs may be at higher risk to be bullied. (HRSA)
- Studies show that 15-25% of US students are bullied with some frequency and 15-20% report that they bully others with some frequency. (HRSA)
- Children and youth who are bullied are more likely to have low self esteem, depression, loneliness and anxiety. (HRSA)

According to the National Youth Prevention Resource Center (NYPRC), both male and female say they are bullied about the way they look or talk. But males are more likely to report being hit, slapped or pushed and females are more likely than males to report to being targets of gossip or sexual comments. Females usually bully girls using more subtle and indirect forms of aggression than boys.

HOW DO YOU MAKE A BULLY STOP?

Bullying can take many different manifestations; therefore, there can be different ways to handle certain situations.

Situation 1: You are being physically bullied:

1. Try not to show any anger or fear. Students who bully like to see that they can upset you.
2. Don't fight back. Don't try to bully others who bully you. Instead, tell the person to stop and walk away.
3. TELL A TRUSTED ADULT! THIS IS THE MOST IMPORTANT!!!!! YOU ARE NOT BEING A TATTLE!!!

Situation 2: You are being cyber bullied:

1. Tell the person to stop.
2. If they don't you should try and block them from accessing whatever online facility you are using.

3. If this does not work and you feel harassed you should tell a trusted adult!!! In many states, there are laws against cyber bullying.

Situation 3: You are being verbally bullied:

1. Try to use humor if you can. If someone tells you that your shoes are ugly then you could say, "Yes, I think their a little goofy looking too."
2. This may not always work, but you should remain calm and not let whoever is bullying you know that they are affecting you.
3. When they say something mean, look them straight in the eye and say, "That wasn't nice. Please stop."
4. If these tactics don't work, talk to a trusted adult. They will be able to help.

Situation 4: You are being verbally bullied, but not to your face:

1. If you know someone is spreading rumors about you, do not hesitate to politely and casually bring up that they should stop talking about you.
2. Never get mad and yell at the bully, it will only make it worse.
3. If you are being socially excluded or gossiped about, and it won't stop, you should talk to a trusted adult. This type of behavior is not ok and it should be addressed.
4. FYI: the above ideas will not make the problem worse. I have tried this method and it is very effective.

WHAT YOU CAN DO?

Next time you see somebody getting bullied, don't just watch. Tell the bully to stop. If the bully sees that his or her peers no longer think that what he or she is doing is funny, they may stop. Also, don't be afraid to tell an adult about bullying you have witnessed. Often, the victim needs help but may be too afraid to seek help. Also, you should talk to your school coordinator about giving lectures and getting involved with anti-bullying programs. Remember that even the smallest thing can make a difference. Just reaching out to a bullying victim can make all the difference in their life. You never know how your actions may affect another.

FOR THE 'RENTS (I.E. PARENTS):

Bullying isn't just something that can be ignored. Often, parents overlook the problem when their child comes to them. Bullying is not just a fact of life and doesn't have to be tolerated. If a child comes to you with a problem it is most likely because it is past the point of ignoring. If they could just ignore it, they wouldn't be asking you for help! Remember, no one should EVER feel alone with this problem.

HERE ARE SOME TIPS:

- Do not dismiss your child or expect them to work the problem out alone. TAKE BULLYING COMPLAINTS SERIOUSLY!!!!
- Praise your child for reporting bullying to you and tell them that you will take action.
- Talk to your youngster's teacher, counselor or other caregiver about any reports of bullying. DO NOT confront the bully's parents or peers.
- Ask your child specific questions about how he or she is treated by peers, who he or she eats with at lunch and how the other children are treated.
- Teach your young one to be assertive. The child should be able to express his or her feelings very well without being aggressive or yelling.

- Identify some of your young one's interests and encourage them to join clubs, sports, or other group activities so they can meet more friends.
- Teach your child to identify bullying behavior and manage them.
- Teach them about how not to be a "not so innocent bystander."
- Let your child know that you do not tolerate bullying behavior.
- Be a positive role model!

The following resources were used for the above information:

1. U.S. Department of Health and Human Services, Health Resources and Service Administration (HRSA); *Stop Bullying Now*
2. National Youth Violence Prevention Resource Center (NYVPRC); *Bullying Facts and Statistics*
3. National Crime Prevention Council (NCPC); *Bullying*

THE LEGAL SIDE OF BULLYING

To stop the growing trend of violence and bullying, it is important to understand laws which have been passed and legal definitions of assault, battery and harassment.

STATE ANTI-BULLYING LAWS:

As of 2008, at least 17 states in the U.S. have passed laws addressing bullying among school children, and many others have considered legislation. They are Arkansas, California, Colorado, Connecticut, Georgia, Illinois, Louisiana, New Hampshire, New Jersey, New York, Oklahoma, Oregon, Rhode Island, Vermont, Virginia, Washington and West Virginia. Most laws have been in effect since 2001. Their passage was motivated, at least in part, by tragic shootings at several U.S.

high schools in the late 1990's and later reports that many perpetrators of school shootings had felt bullied or threatened by peers.

HOW IS BULLYING DEFINED IN STATE LAWS?

1. Three states (Arkansas, New Jersey and Oregon) require districts to establish a definition of "bullying." In eleven states, bullying is defined in law.
2. Several states do not define bullying in their state laws. Those that do define the term vary in the types of behaviors that constitute bullying.

Examples include:

Colorado: Any written or verbal expression, or physical act or gesture, or a pattern thereof that is intended to cause distress upon one or more students.

Georgia: Any willful attempt or threat to inflict injury on another person... or any intentional display of force such as would give the victim reason to fear or expect immediate bodily harm.

Some state laws equate bullying with harassment and intimidation.

STATE LEGISLATIVE FINDINGS ABOUT BULLYING:

Several states include legislative findings about bullying in their laws. Legislative findings reflect the seriousness with which policymakers consider the issue.

Examples include:

New Jersey: Bullying, like other disruptive or violent behaviors...disrupts both a student's ability to learn and a school's ability to educate its students in a safe environment.

Vermont: Students who are continually filled with apprehension and anxiety are unable to learn and unlikely to succeed.

The "how to do this for states" - a comprehensive state anti-bullying policy should include the following components:

- Defines bullying
- Prohibits bullying by students
- Informs students and others of anti-bullying policy
- Enables students and parents to report bullying incidents
- Requires teachers and school staff to report bullying incidents
- Provides immunity to those reporting bullying incidents and protection from reprisal, retaliation or false accusations against victims or witnesses with information regarding bullying
- Requires administrators to investigate reported incidents
- Encourages or requires bullying prevention in schools

The anti-bullying laws in Connecticut, New Jersey, Oregon, Vermont and West Virginia contain all of the above components.

CYBERBULLYING LAWS:

Cyberbullying is a term often used to describe Internet bullying. It is often difficult to pass laws for cyberbullying because any anti-cyberbullying law would restrict free speech and potential anti-cyberbullying laws must comply with the exceptions to First Amendment protection. A handful of states passed cyberbullying laws in 2007, yet these laws only dealt with cyberbullying in schools. A number of states, including Missouri and Pennsylvania, currently have pending legislation concerning the criminalization of cyberbullying. The Missouri bill would make it a felony when a person twenty-one years old or older harasses a person seventeen years or younger.

A number of states, such as California, have passed anti-cyberstalking laws. Cyberstalking often includes credible threats both online and offline, while cyberbullying usually does not. Although the problem of cyberbullying is escalating, parents still do not have the legal means to remove defamatory materials from the Internet. Therefore, children who are victims of cyberbullying have no legal course of action to remove offensive materials—they are left to be humiliated and taunted for months and possibly even years.

HOW CAN YOU HELP?

It is difficult, but it can be done. Sensitive laws and policies can be developed to address bullying in U.S. schools and to encourage support and effective bullying prevention and intervention programs in schools.

It is a challenge and many states have issued policies and provided technical support to help educators in the interpretation and implementation of laws. If your state has not passed anti-bullying laws, talk to your state representatives about bullying and encourage them to pass laws and develop programs to protect our children!

Although states may not have passed specific laws for anti-bullying and cyberbullying, this does not mean you have no recourse if someone is physically or verbally assaulting and harassing you. Under the federal and state laws of the United States Government, you have protection and this is why you need to understand the legal definitions of assault, battery, assault and battery, and harassment.

LEGAL DEFINITIONS OF ASSAULT, BATTERY, ASSAULT AND BATTERY, AND HARASSMENT:

How many times have our youth been verbally harassed, hit, pushed, kicked or physically harmed by another person? At times we think it is something all children go through when growing up; an issue to deal with, and then move on. Did you know these actions could be classified by our federal and state government as assault, battery, assault and battery, or harassment and are against the law? There is something you can do when you are being bullied in this manner and you don't have to suffer in silence! You can say, "Hey, stop it! That's against the law!" Please read the following legal definitions to understand why bullying is a criminal issue.

Assault: It is a crime, defined as any attempt or threat to injure another person. An assault is committed without physical contact. It is any display of force that the victim has reason to fear and expect bodily harm. Example: on the bus, if Wayne would have raised his hand to hit Dorie, but then changed his mind and didn't hit her; it still would be considered a criminal offense of assault. Also, for an assault to be a crime the victim does not need to be afraid if the outward gesture is threatening and defendant intends harm.

Battery: It is a crime, defined as unlawful application of force to another person. Battery requires physical contact of some sort (bodily injury or offensive touching) without justification or excuse. Example: when Dorie was tripped and hit on the bus—it was a criminal offense of battery.

Assault and Battery: This is serious business and in most jurisdictions, laws have been created for aggravated assaults (assault committed with the intention of committing some additional crime) and batteries and they are punishable as felonies.

Harassment: It is a crime, defined as words, gestures and actions which tend to annoy, alarm and abuse (verbally) another person. Example: on the bus, when Dana was saying really mean things to Dorie, she was harassing her, but I need to be honest and say when Dorie blew up and said things to Dana, she was also harassing her.

FINAL THOUGHTS ON BULLYING AND HOW CAN WE MAKE CHANGES:

Bullying has become a tidal wave of epic proportions. Although bullying was once considered a rite of passage, parents, educators, and community leaders now see bullying as a devastating form of abuse that can have long term effects on youthful victims, robbing them of self-esteem, isolating them from their peers, causing them to drop out of school, and even prompting health problems and suicide. (NCRC)

While approaches that simply crack down on individual bullies are seldom effective, when there is a school-wide commitment to end bullying, it can be reduced by up to 50%. One approach that has been shown to be effective focuses on changing school and classroom climates by: raising awareness about bullying, increasing teacher and parent involvement and supervision, forming clear rules and strong social norms against bullying, and providing support and protection for all students. Adults need to become aware of the extent of bullying at school and they need to involve themselves in changing the situation, rather than looking the other way. Students also need to pledge not to bully other students and to help students who are bullied, and to make a point to include students who are left out. (NYVPRC)

EATING DISORDER FACT SHEET

The following information was obtained from:

1. National Institute of Mental Health (NIMH); *Eating Disorders*
2. United States Department of Health and Human Resources–Substance Abuse and Mental Health Services Administration, National Mental Health Information Center (SAMHSA); *Eating Disorders*
3. National Eating Disorders Association; *What Should I Say? Tips for Talking to a Friend Who May Be Struggling With an Eating Disorder;* (www.NationalEatingDisorders.org)

WHAT IS AN EATING DISORDER?

Eating Disorders often are long-term illnesses that may require long-term treatment. In addition, eating disorders frequently occur with other mental disorders such as depression, substance abuse, and anxiety disorders. The earlier these disorders are diagnosed and treated, the better the chances are for full recovery. Research shows that more than 90 percent of those who have eating disorders are women between the ages of 12 and 25. Did you know that there are 8,000,000 or more people in the U.S. who have an eating disorder!!

Also, eating disorders usually start with teens but they can start as young as 8 years old!! This may seem very shocking and it may seem like a large number unless you understand the definition of eating disorders. There are three types; anorexia nervosas, bulimia nervosas, and binge eating. People with **anorexia** are obsessed with being thin and often skip meals or are extremely obsessive about their food. Because of this, people suffering with anorexia often appear too thin and sometimes malnourished. **Bulimia** is like anorexia except the person afflicted will vomit their food. They often follow the binge/purge cycle. In the binge/purge cycle they eat a lot and then throw it up. The third eating disorder, **binge eating**, is found evenly between men and women. Binge eaters gorge themselves with food, like bulimia, except they don't throw it up. Binge eaters often feel really guilty about what they do and it is often done in private and fairly quickly.

If you are saying, "What is so bad about an eating disorder? I just want to look thin!" You should read this!!!!

THE DANGERS OF EATING DISORDERS:

- Death
- Heart disease
- Depression
- Suicidal thoughts or behavior
- Loss of your period or an extremely irregular cycle (in some cases you can lose your ability to have children)
- Bone loss
- Stunted growth
- Nerve damage
- Seizures
- Digestive problems
- Bowel irregularities
- Tooth decay
- Ruptured esophagus
- High blood pressure
- Type 2 diabetes
- Gallbladder disease

These are serious health problems and some of them can be life threatening!!!!! Now you know what an eating disorder is and you know what it can do to your body, so are you wondering if you have one? Do not fear because for your convenience, I have added a personal test and you can use the information to verify if you or somebody else possibly has an eating disorder.

EATING DISORDER TEST:

1. Do you constantly calculate numbers of fat grams and calories?

   ☐ Yes   ☐ No

2. Do you weigh yourself often and find yourself obsessed with the number on the scale?

   ☐ Yes   ☐ No

3. Do you exercise to burn off calories and not for health enjoyment?

   ☐ Yes   ☐ No

4. Do you ever feel out of control when you are eating?

   ☐ Yes   ☐ No

5. Do your eating patterns include extreme dieting, preferences for certain foods, withdraw or ritualized behavior at mealtime or secretive bingeing?

   ☐ Yes   ☐ No

6. Have weight loss, dieting, and/or control of food become one of your major priorities?

   ☐ Yes   ☐ No

7. Do you feel ashamed, disgusted or guilty after eating?

   ☐ Yes   ☐ No

8. Do you constantly worry about weight, shape or size of your body?

   ☐ Yes   ☐ No

9. Do you feel like your identity and value is based on how you look or how much you weigh?

☐ Yes   ☐ No

10. Have any of your peers tried to talk with you about having an eating disorder?

☐ Yes   ☐ No

If you answered "yes" to any of these questions, then you may have an eating disorder. Admitting you have a problem may be very hard so you should talk to a trusted adult or even your doctor. It is a serious problem and won't "just go away" on its own, but it is curable, so please ask for help. If you don't know anyone to talk with you can always contact the hotlines I have listed below.

Did you pass the test, but are now worried somebody you know may have an eating disorder? Here are a few signs to look for:

SIGNS OF AN EATING DISORDER:

- Depression
- Anxiety
- Obsessive behavior
- Substance abuse
- Cardiovascular problems
- Impaired physical developments
- Thinning of the bones
- Brittle hair or nails
- Dry or yellowish skin, often flaky
- Growth of fine hair all over body, including face
- Muscle weakness
- Fainting
- Severe constipation
- Person feels cold all the time

- Slow breathing and pulse
- You are able to clearly see a lot of bones on the body (they protrude)
- The person throws up after meals or always goes to the bathroom after meals, and afterwards, their breath smells of vomit
- The person often lies about eating meals and if everyone is eating, they may say that they already ate
- The person is always talking about their weight and calorie intake
- The person is exercising constantly
- Chronically inflamed soar throat
- Swollen glands in the neck and below the jaw
- Decaying and sensitive teeth
- Intestinal distress and irritation from laxative use
- Severe dehydration from purging

This is a very long list and if your friend has more than two or three of these symptoms, then you may want to have a talk. Tell your friend it's "ok" and encourage them to seek help. Unfortunately, people with eating disorders often do not want to admit their problem and will deny it. Do not feel afraid or ashamed to talk with their parents or a trusted adult about the situation. They will be able to help and find someone to fully diagnose the problem.

Let's say you don't have an eating disorder and you are wondering, why someone would ever want to deprive themselves of food or eat too much food? There are quite a few factors contributing to eating disorders and learning about them will help you protect yourself from this dangerous disease.

FACTORS THAT CONTRIBUTE TO AN EATING DISORDER:

Physiological factors:

- Low self-esteem

- Feelings of inadequacy or lack of control in life
- Depression, anxiety, anger, or loneliness

Interpersonal factors:

- Troubled family and personal relationships
- Difficulty expressing emotions or feelings
- History of being ridiculed based on size or weight
- History of physical or sexual abuse

Social Factors:

- Cultural pressures that glorify thinness and place a value on obtaining the perfect body
- Narrow definitions of beauty that include only women and men of specific body weights and shapes
- Cultural norms that value people on the basis of physical appearance and not inner strengths.

After reading these points, I hope you realize your actions have a huge impact on others around you!! America, it appears, has turned into a country based on the looks of people and not the qualities of people. Look at how magazines make fun of celebrities because their body size is different from what the media considers fashionable!! It's ridiculous! I am 5'10", weigh 160 pounds and I am in great physical shape. I am proud of this because I am healthy and you should be proud of yourself too. It is difficult when the media surrounds us with computer generated photos of models and tells us we have to look like these photos to be beautiful. It is not true and we don't have to support these myths!!!! Don't buy products and publications that degrade you and make you feel worse about yourself!!! There is more to life than our looks and size, instead, buy things that empower and celebrate the differences of people. Your mind and body will thank you in the end. Remember, outer beauty is fleeting, but inner beauty is everlasting!

HOTLINES FOR HELP:

1. National Association of Anorexia Nervosa and Associated
    Disorders
    Hotline: 1-847-831-3438
    Web address: www.anad.org

2. National Eating Disorders Association
    Hotline: 1-800-931-2237
    Web address: www.NationalEatingDisorders.org

RESOURCES

SUGGESTED BULLYING WEBSITES FOR PARENTS AND YOUTH:

www.stopbullingnow.hrsa.gov; U.S. Department of Health and Human Services, Health Resources and Service Administration (HRSA)

www.safeyouth.org; National Youth Violence Prevention Resource Center (NYVPRC)

www.mentalhealth.samhsa.gov; United States Department of Health and Human Services—Substance Abuse and Mental Health Services Administration, National Mental Health Information Center (SAMHSA)

wwww.ncpc.org; National Crime Prevention Council (NCPC)

HOTLINES FOR HELP:

National Center for Victims of Crime
1-800-FYI-CALL (394-2255)
Email: gethelp@ncvc.org

National Suicide Prevention Lifeline
1-800-273-TALK (8255)
Available 24 hours; immediate assistances for those in a suicide crisis

National Hopeline Network
1-800-SUICIDE (784-2433)
www.hopeline.com
Connects people who are depressed, suicidal, or concerned about someone they love

National Domestic Violence Hotline
1-800-799-SAFE (7233) or 1-800-787-3224
Hotline for victims of domestic and family violence at home and for concerned observers

National Child Abuse Hotline
1-800-4-A-CHILD (1-800-422-4453)
A hotline for someone worried that child abuse is occurring

National Sexual Assault Hotline
1-800-656-HOPE (4673)
Connects sexual assault victims to crisis centers

National Runaway Switchboard
1-800-RUNAWAY (621-4000)
For runaway youth/teens in crisis and concerned family/friends.

Girls and Boys Town Hotline
1-800-448-3000 or 1-800-448-1833
Email: hotline@boystown.org
Available 24 hours; for crisis, staffed by trained counselors.

Covenant House "Nineline"
1-800-999-9999 or 1-800-999-9915
Available 24 hours; serves runaway and homeless youth and also operates as a hotline for kids and parents with any kind of problem

National Center for Missing and Exploited Children
1-800-THE-LOST (1-800-843-5678)
www.missingkids.com
For families and law enforcements seeking children who are missing, or to report a missing child

National Eating Disorders Association
1-800-931-2237
Eating disorders
www.NationalEatingDisorders.org

National Association of Anorexia and Associated Disorders
1-847-831-3438
Eating Diorders
web address: www.anad.org

Add your own hotlines for help here:

Name: _____

Number: _____

Web site address: _____

Name: _____

Number: _____

Web site address: _____

Name: _____

Number: _____

Web site address: _____

Name: _____

Number: _____

Web site address: _____

Name: _____

Number: _____

Web site address: _____

Name: _____

Number: _____

Web site address: _____

NOTES

BIOGRAPHIES

The Author

Brigitte Berman was born in February of 1994. She currently lives in a suburban town in Massachusetts with her parents, sister and two adored dogs. Brigitte is an avid reader and loves to explore different types of music with the violin, piano and her newest hobby, the electric guitar. Even though Brigitte would never be asked to join an Olympic Team, she still enjoys a large variety of sports. She excitedly pursues interests such as the Astronomy Club and Robotics Club and encourages other girls to become involved in science. During the middle of Brigitte's eighth grade year, she realized something needed to be done about bullying because it seemed to be everywhere in today's world. She started laying plans for her book in January of 2008 by doing research through focus groups with her questionnaires and online survey. During the summer, she wrote the majority of her book before entering ninth grade. It is her hope and aspiration to be able to help young adults throughout America and to raise awareness of the devastation from bullying. For more information, please visit Brigitte's website at doriewitt.com.

The Cover Artist

Howie Green came to national attention with the publication of his book *Jazz Fish Zen: Adventures in Mamboland*, which became a category best-seller and has developed a global cult following. As a graphic designer, multimedia and web designer and illustrator Howie has won over 40 awards for his work. Howie is an internationally recognized Pop Art painter and his work has been featured in over 30 solo and group art gallery shows and he has painted over 20 public and private murals. Three of Howie's painted life-sized cows were featured in the 2006 Boston Cows Parade. For more information or to see Howie's art, visit his web site: www.hgd.com.

189

Dorie Dorie Dorie

Dorie Dorie Dorie

Dorie Dorie Dorie